AUSTRALIAN HISTORY IN 7 QUESTIONS

AUSTRALIAN HISTORY IN 7 QUESTIONS

JOHN HIRST

Published by Black Inc.,
an imprint of Schwartz Publishing Pty Ltd
37–39 Langridge Street
Collingwood Vic 3066 Australia
email: enquiries@blackincbooks.com
http://www.blackincbooks.com

National Library of Australia Cataloguing-in-Publication entry:

Hirst, J. B. (John Bradley), 1942– author.
Australian history in 7 questions / John Hirst.
9781863956703 (paperback)
9781922231703 (ebook)
Australia—History.
994

Cover design: Peter Long

Cover images: *The Founding of Australia* by Algernon Talmage (1937), used with permission of the State Library of NSW (call no. ML 1222); Getty Images.

Map design: MAPgraphics Pty Ltd

CONTENTS

INTRODUCTION

I KNOW THAT MANY PEOPLE FIND AUSTRALIAN history dull and predictable. They get too much of it at school and if they are still interested in history at adulthood they turn with relief to *The Tudors* on the BBC and to the books of Simon Schama, Niall Ferguson or Jared Diamond.

I was conscious of the challenge I faced when a branch of the University of the Third Age in Melbourne asked me to lecture on Australian history. I had lectured with success to several branches on European history, repeating the lectures I gave at university and which became the book *The Shortest History of Europe*. How could I match that for Australian history? I offered four lectures under the heading 'Four Questions in Australian History'. If there are genuine questions about Australian history, there is something to puzzle over. The history ceases to be predictable—and dull. These lectures too were well received, which encouraged me to add a few more questions and make a book in this style.

By this route I have reached the same point as I did when considering how best to present European history. In both cases I have departed from a straightforward narrative in favour of a more thematic treatment. Narrative can make history a good read, but it can also leave unanswered the questions 'What makes this society distinctive?' and 'Why did its history take this course?'

The answers to the questions that this book poses can be read separately. Taken together, I hope they provide as good a guide to Australian society as the more orthodox histories, or an even better one. It is unquestionably a much shorter book than the usual.

I owe a debt to that excellent institution the University of the Third Age for setting me on this path. Lotte Mulligan, who was a colleague when we were both at La Trobe University, now has a second academic life as the organiser of studies at the Stonnington branch of the University of the Third Age. She has been a great supporter of my efforts and the chief urger for this book to be written. To her my thanks.

Question 1 is new territory for me. I am very grateful to Professor Peter Bellwood of the Australian National University, a world expert in this field, for looking over and correcting my chapter. Professor Ann McGrath, also at the Australian National University and a former student of mine, helped me with Aboriginal life in the Northern Territory. I talked over James Belich's book on the Anglo-world with Professor Graeme Davison, and he kindly read Chapter 3.

John Hirst
December 2013

QUESTION 1
WHY DID ABORIGINES NOT BECOME FARMERS?

I N THE BEGINNING ALL HUMANKIND WERE hunter-gatherers. About 10,000 BC agriculture was developed independently in a handful of places around the globe. It then spread widely; it came close to Australia, but in Aboriginal times was not established here. The Aborigines remained hunter-gatherers.

The highlands of New Guinea were one of the places where agriculture was developed, but it did not spread far, not even to the whole of the island. China was another place of agricultural invention, and from there it spread south to the Philippines and then west to Indonesia and eastward into the Pacific. So Timor, New Guinea, the Solomons, Vanuatu and Fiji had fields and gardens and settled village life. Australians now call this part of the globe an 'arc of instability'. In prehistoric times these were places of settled life, while the Australian Aborigines remained wanderers.

Gardens came very close to Australia; they were cultivated on islands in the Torres Strait, between Australia and New Guinea. The people here were Melanesian, like the other gardeners in this region, though most spoke an Australian Aboriginal language. As this suggests, the Aborigines of Cape York had close relations with the gardeners of the Torres Strait – so close that the fuzzier hair of the Melanesians is found quite a way down Cape York.

The Cape York Aborigines traded and fought with the Torres Strait Islanders. The islanders took heads from the Aborigines they had killed to trade for outrigger canoes from New Guinea. The Aborigines, in turn, traded with the islanders to obtain canoes so they had more sophisticated craft than the bark canoes that were used in other parts of Australia. The Aborigines followed some of the rituals of the islanders: they used drums in their ceremonies and placed the corpses of the dead on platforms. The islanders learnt of the throwing stick, or woomera, from the Aborigines.

In all this exchange the Aborigines learnt about gardens and garden crops, but they did not become gardeners. Sometimes it is said that Australia's soil and climate and its plants were not suitable for agriculture, but this argument won't work for Cape York. The soil and climate were the same as on the islands. The women on Cape York dug up the same yams that were planted in gardens in Torres Strait. Coconut trees grow wild in Cape York but were not planted as they were on the islands.

From around 1700 AD the Aborigines in Arnhem Land and the Kimberleys were exposed to rice, one of the standard agricultural crops, first developed in China. The Macassans from the island of Sulawesi in Indonesia sailed each year to the Australian coast to collect trepang, or sea cucumber, which they sold for use in China—as a food and as an aphrodisiac. They brought rice to live on during their stay in Australia and to supply to the Aborigines, with whom they wanted to remain on good terms while they camped on their territory. The Aborigines liked rice, and the Aboriginal men who went back to Sulawesi with the Macassans for the off-season saw rice being grown, but the Aborigines did not move to cultivate their own rice. It could be done. The Chinese grew rice in the Northern Territory in European times.

The Europeans who came to Australia had an easy answer for the failure of the Aborigines to develop farming: they were a backward people. In their understanding, the progress of humankind could be marked by the movement from hunter-gathering to herding, then to agriculture, to trading and finally to manufacturing. As racial ideas firmed up during the nineteenth century, Aborigines became still more inferior in European eyes. Instead of being a backward people who might yet improve, they were branded a congenitally inferior race that was incapable of advancing. We have ditched the notion of racial differences, but we might still be tempted to think of

Aborigines as backward, since the civilisation we inhabit is a result of the development of agriculture and all that it made possible. Over the last fifty or so years, anthropologists and archaeologists have been accumulating the evidence to drive that idea out of our heads.

You think the Aborigines were backward? Watch them trapping ducks on the Murray River. They stretch a long net across the river, just above the water. They disturb a group of ducks grazing on the river a little distance away. The ducks fly along the river towards the net. Should they start flying too high, one of the hunters throws a bark disc over them and gives a shrill whistle like a hawk. The ducks dip down—and fly into the net. The explorer Thomas Mitchell examined one of these nets and declared that the fibre and weaving were as good as any made in Britain.

You think of Aborigines as incapable of development? At about the same time that agriculture was spreading through South-east Asia (4500 to 3500 years ago), the Aborigines began using resources in a more intense way—which provided for a greater population, the same result which agriculture brought. Archaeologists map this change by the greater number of campsites they uncover from this period, the signs of more people using them, the appearance of new foods in the diet and new technology like fishhooks made from shell, the exploitation of offshore islands for the first time, and, most surprising of all, the appearance in a few places of houses and a more settled life. The most substantial settlement was at Lake Condah, in western Victoria, where the Aborigines built stone houses beside the network of waterways they had constructed to store and trap eels.

If agriculture is the test of development, something like agriculture was practised by the Aborigines in the interior of the continent. They could colonise this harsh country because they learnt to harvest the native grass, nardoo. The grass was cut and stacked in stooks to dry. Thomas Mitchell said the scene looked like a hayfield in England. The nardoo seeds were knocked out of the stalks, the chaff was blown away, and the seeds were ground into flour with a rock on a grinding stone. The flour was then baked into cakes in the ashes of the fire. In their last days on Coopers Creek, the explorers Burke and Wills ground nardoo seeds into flour, in an effort to keep themselves alive, something they had learnt from the Aborigines.

The archaeologist Rhys Jones did most to jog our thinking about how Aborigines got their living when he coined the term 'firestick farming'. Aborigines regularly set fire to the country, which kept it open and brought on fresh grass that attracted kangaroos and other animals. The British regularly were amazed to find much of the country so open, a scattering of trees with no underbrush, and looking like an English gentleman's park, which was a very contrived landscape. It was the Aborigines who had contrived to make Australia like this, and hence ready to be used by the British for their sheep and cattle.

Burning the land is not, of course, close and careful cultivation, but the historian Bill Gammage in a major recent book, *The Biggest Estate on Earth,* argues that Aborigines did not simply set the country alight, they also micromanaged fire to make a patchwork of different environments suitable for the animals and plants they wanted to exploit. His argument has been contested, and it overlooks the carelessness of Aborigines with fire. They never put out a campfire, and if they wanted to freshen up a firestick they would put it in dry grass, get the flame they wanted on the firestick, and leave the grass burning.

Gammage has also argued that the Aboriginal treatment of plants should be called farming. Those wide swathes of native grasses must have been weeded. Yam grounds were pre-served, and the top part of the yam replanted so that it would grow again. But the Aborigines never domesticated a plant by careful breeding and re-sowing, which is part of what is meant by agriculture.

For all that Gammage wants to insist that Aborigines were engaged in farming, he does make this important concession: 'People farmed in 1788 (and before) but were not farmers.' Being a farmer is to follow a settled life, and Aborigines wanted to be on the move, connecting with all parts of their land, which had sacred significance to them. It was their failure to settle any-where permanently which convinced the British that Aborigines were at the lowest level of human development. When Captain Cook anchored in Botany Bay in 1770 he saw only rude bark shelters and a wandering people who did not cultivate the soil. Had he seen stone houses like those at Lake Condah, the British government would not have been so confident that they did not have to buy land for their convict settlement from the Aborigines or make a treaty with them. They had made treaties with the American Indians and would make a treaty with the Maori of New Zealand. When West Africa was being considered for the convict settlement, the planning included the purchase of land from the natives.

In 1992 the Australian High Court, in the *Mabo* case, overturned 200 years of legal history and declared that native title did exist in Australia. Where the land had been sold or leased, native title had been extinguished, but elsewhere, if the Aborigines could show an ongoing traditional attachment to their land, they held native title over it. The case which led to this ruling did not concern Aborigines on the mainland; Eddie Mabo and his fellow plaintiffs held gardening land on Murray Island, in the Torres Strait, which was a late addition to Australia.

The British government claimed the islands in the Torres Strait in 1879. They became part of Queensland, and in 1901, with federation, part of Australia. The British government was concerned with security and lawlessness in the strait; it had no intention of promoting European settlement there. The gardeners remained on their land, and a local court on Murray Island settled disputes over land ownership in the traditional way. The legal team running the *Mabo* case was delighted to find some old court records under banana leaves in a disused hut.

The case for these gardeners having a traditional right to their land was strong, but landholding and land use by the hunter-gatherers on the mainland was very different. The purpose of the progressive lawyers who brought this case was to establish native title throughout Australia. They became worried that they had almost too good a case: what if the court declared for the survival of native title on the islands but not on the mainland?

They need not have worried. The High Court was looking to make a landmark ruling, and it rejected the notion that the rights of indigenous people to land depended on the stage of their development, whether they were hunters or cultivators of the soil. That was the notion held in 1788; it could not be accepted in modern Australia. If indigenous people were occupying land, they held a native title to it, no matter how they were getting their living. It mattered so little that the court did not declare that Eddie Mabo was the owner of his land: it declared that the Murray people owned their island.

The court did not question the British government's claiming sovereignty over Australia; the mistake in our legal history was to suppose that sovereignty made the government the owners of all the land, which it could sell without reference to the Aborigines. The court was envisaging an alternative history for Australia, in which the government would have negotiated with the Aborigines for the use or sale of land. Like the High Court judges, many people of goodwill think that relations with Aborigines would have been altogether different if treaties had been made with them.

However, it is easier to make treaties with a settled people than with hunter-gatherers. The Aborigines had no paramount chief to negotiate with. They had no notion that their land could be sold. They were intimately connected with all parts of it: they belonged to it, rather than it to them. They did have a notion of allowing other people to use their land temporarily for a specific purpose.

On the one occasion when a treaty was concluded, the Aborigines probably assumed they were making an agreement of this sort. The treaty was offered in 1835 by John Batman and his party, freelance adventurers from Tasmania, who wanted to run sheep around Port Phillip in what is now Victoria. The treaty was concluded somewhere just north of the present site of Melbourne. In return for the ownership of a large swathe of country, Batman promised the Aborigines an annual payment of blankets, knives, tomahawks, clothing, looking glasses, scissors and flour. The British government disowned the treaty: it did not want settlement to extend into this region, and it claimed the sole right to dispose of land. The pastoralists nevertheless kept coming and there was no treaty.

Batman, like all the other pioneer pastoralists, wanted more than temporary use of the land for his livestock. Even if some agreements could have been reached with the Aborigines, powerful sources of conflict would have remained: the Aborigines would have 'stolen' sheep thinking that the Europeans should share their abundance with them, and Europeans who had sex with Aboriginal women (who were often offered to them) would not have realised that they had incurred obligations to the women's kin.

The most effective way for an indigenous people to make invaders deal with them was to successfully resist their advance. The Maori of New Zealand and the Indians in the United States were only subdued by the use of regular military units. But the hunter-gatherers of Australia could not mount such a defence of their territories.

Aborigines lived day by day in small bands; they rarely came together in larger groupings. There were over 500 tribes in Australia, which spoke different languages and were often hostile to one another. Aborigines were warriors but their battles were more like raids and skirmishes. Large formations in the field for a long time was not their way and was beyond their capacity. They fought over women and the sorcery practised against them by their neighbours, but not for territory. It took them some time to realise that the Europeans wanted to take land from them.

At first the Aborigines avoided the Europeans or attempted to assimilate them into their society. Their violence was not intended to repel the invaders but to make them behave properly. By the time they realised what the Europeans wanted, they were usually overwhelmed by the number of invaders or devastated by the diseases they brought. When they did make a fight of it, they were brought under control by bands of settlers, contingents of mounted police and by the native police, who were used regularly in Queensland, where resistance was strongest. The native police were Aborigines recruited from outside the region who were keen to slaughter foreign Aborigines. Soldiers were used in small numbers against the Aborigines, but never armies, and their resistance was never so strong that governments considered treating with them.

The significance for our history since 1788 of the indigenous population being hunter-gatherers should now be plain. No treaties; the hunting grounds open to pastoral invasion; no strong resistance. So why did the Aborigines remain hunter-gatherers? Our opening question has not been forgotten.

*

The Australian Aborigines were not unusual in spurning agriculture when it was on offer: most hunter-gathering groups round the globe preferred to remain that way. Agriculture spread in part because the first farmers moved into the territory of the hunter-gatherers, displacing them, marginalising them or forcing them to join them. Agriculture came to the arc of islands around northern Australia (though not New Guinea) with the spread of the Austronesian people from the north. Today, all the peoples in an immensely wide area—from Madagascar, off the African coast, to Indonesia and the islands of the Pacific—speak related languages (Austronesian) because they are descendants of the one farming people.

THE ADVANCE OF THE AUSTRONESIANS

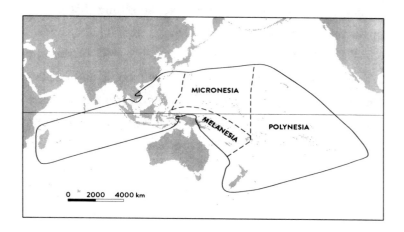

But in other parts of the globe it is harder to assign agriculture to the arrival of farmers—or, at least, to their overwhelming presence. By some means or other, over a long period hunting people moved to agriculture, without at first giving up on hunting. How much the spread of farming relied on the movement of farmers and how much by osmosis, as it were, is a matter of great contention among prehistorians. But no one thinks that an intact hunter-gathering society would move rapidly to agriculture, seizing it in a moment as clearly a superior way of life.

In the first place, it is not obviously superior. Hunters and gatherers could live well. As Geoffrey Blainey says, when the Europeans came to Australia the Aborigines probably had a better standard of living than European peasants. Enough food could be gained by a few hours' work each day. There was plenty of leisure time for ritual, intrigue and play. Blainey calls the Aborigines 'the prosperous nomads'. Agriculture required more hours and harder work, and very soon it allowed for social differentiation between those who owned the land and those who worked it.

It is the barriers to the embracing of agriculture which are now more strongly stressed by scholars—which makes the first moves to agriculture the more puzzling. Hunter-gatherers share food and resources among kin; if an individual farmer and his family are to labour in planting and harvesting and storing a crop, those communal ties will have to have been broken or weakened. In modern Australia the strength of these ties among traditional Aborigines is still strong—and still a barrier to individual enterprise. What is the point of getting a job or starting a business if you have to share your earnings with your relatives? The Aboriginal artists, whose paintings sell for top dollar, do not become rich; they give their earnings away and live on the dole or a pension like the rest of the community.

The move from hunting to cropping cannot be thought of simply as moving from one way of getting food to another. The animals and plants that supported the hunter-gatherers were closely interconnected with their social and religious life. In Aboriginal society a man could not eat his totem (say, a kangaroo) and was responsible for the ceremonies to sponsor its increase. Some foods were forbidden to women and children, others eaten only on special occasions. Though Aborigines consumed animals and plants, they respected them as part of the same spirit world they lived in.

To the despair of those who want Aboriginal health to improve today, the Aborigines will not destroy the dogs that multiply in their camps and settlements. It is not for them to determine whether dogs live or die. In the famous 1960s strike that the Gurindji people ran against the cattle company Vesteys in the Northern Territory, the Aboriginal workers were meant to stop the windmills that filled the water troughs where cattle drank. This was the instruction from the white organisers of the strike. The Aborigines stalled on this manoeuvre. Their leader, Vincent Lingiari, said, 'We not bin let them cattle die of thirst. Them big Bestey bosses not hear them cattle die; but I bin hear them cattle die.'

Planting and harvesting crops establishes a very different regime: man is now in charge of nature, not part of it. This represents a fundamental change in mind and culture. How could this change happen in those hunter-gatherers who were the agricultural pioneers? Did it precede the move to agriculture or was it a consequence of the change? Or something of both? This, too, is a matter of dispute—or, better to say, speculation, since there is little evidence.

Graeme Barker, a leading scholar in the field, has assembled a list of thirty-nine explanations that have been offered for the move to agriculture. Some are outlandish, such as the arrival of aliens. Some are contradictory: rich environments (which broke down the sharing ethic) or marginal environments (which impelled the search for more food). Some might be consequences as much as causes (population growth). Some are preconditions rather than causes in themselves, such as climatic change (the warming after the last ice age, which made cultivation possible) or hunters becoming more sedentary (and so looking to have food on hand).

PROFESSOR BARKER'S LIST

Some of the causes that have been proposed for the

transition from foraging to farming:

aliens	natural habitat
big men	natural selection
broad spectrum adaptation	nutritional stress
circumscription	oases
climatic change	plant migration
competition	population growth
desertification	population pressure
diffusion	random genetic kicks
domesticability	resource concentration
energetics	resource pressure
familiarity	rich environments
fat intake	rituals
feasting	scheduling conflicts
geniuses	sedentism
hormones	storage
intelligence	technological innovation
kitchen gardening	water access
land ownership	xenophobia
marginal environments	zoological diversity
multicausal	

These explanations have to be modified, now that there is an acceptance of the mental and social ties that bound hunter-gatherers to their ways of food collecting. It is not enough to say, for example, that food was in short supply so hunters started systematically planting grasses, the predecessors of wheat and barley. Hunter-gatherers did respond to their environment and make rational calculations, but in a very different mental world from our own.

One proposed explanation acknowledges this: hunter-gatherers thought the gods were angry because they had removed the grain from wild grasses—they had reaped the grain spirit—and so they set about replacing the grasses and choosing the best seeds and plants to do so. This is close to the worldview of the Aboriginal women replacing the tops of yams, who say the yam spirit will become angry and not let any more yams grow if this offering is not made. With more time and in different circumstances, the Aboriginal women with this mindset might have become more systematic cultivators of the yam.

If the default position of hunter-gatherers is to remain hunter-gatherers, then we can give this answer to our question: there was no disturbance to push the Aborigines into different ways—just seeing agriculture was certainly not enough—and pioneer farmers did not arrive and compel them to change. The Austronesians seem to have touched on Australian soil. They brought the dingo, which was a late arrival; the founding population of Aborigines did not have it. But although they were great colonisers, they left Australia alone. We are used to explaining why the Dutch discoverers of the west coast did not plan settlements in Australia (they saw only barren territory with no signs of useful products); the lack of interest by the Austronesians is just as important.

*

The British who did settle were agriculturalists, and when they turned their minds to civilising and Christianising the Aborigines, making them into farmers was the top priority. This would compel them to settle in one place, which was thought to be the necessary first step for their advancement.

Governor Macquarie in the 1810s made a determined attempt to set Aborigines up as farmers. The missionaries who ran his schemes failed, and later mission settlements in southern Australia had very little success. To get Aborigines to take any interest in their settlements, the missionaries had to provide them with rations. In time the Aborigines were meant to grow their own food, but they were not interested in the hard, regular work that this required. If the missionaries stopped their rations because they would not work, Aborigines would get their food elsewhere, either by begging from whites (which to them was no shame, since whites had plenty to share), by taking casual jobs or by returning to hunting and gathering. Missionaries were left with children as the only permanent residents, and soon came to believe that only with them did they have any chance of success. They would see the adults only when they had rations to give out.

It was not simply the hard work that put Aborigines off farming. They quickly sussed out the social arrangements of farming: the men who did the hard work were looked down upon and the gentlemen owners got the rewards. As many observers noted, when these semi-naked or fully naked 'savages' thought of themselves in European terms, they considered themselves to be like the gentlemen—men of leisure, basically. At Blacktown, the Aboriginal settlement west of Sydney, six cottages were built for Aboriginal farmers, which remained mostly unoccupied. To the shock of the management committee, the Aborigines asked for convicts to be allocated to them to do the farming work! Of course this was regarded as preposterous. Those who wanted to bring Aborigines into European society assumed they must work hard and join the lower orders.

The difficulty with any scheme of advancement was that the Aborigines had no wish to live in the European way, with an abundance of possessions. They did not envy the Europeans their possessions, unlike the native peoples of the Pacific. Since Aborigines had few wants, they were not going to do work they did not like. This brought despair to the missionaries. Captain Cook had been a more sympathetic observer:

> From what I have said of the natives of New Holland they
> may appear to some to be the most wretched people upon
> the earth: but in reality they are far more happier than we
> Europeans; being wholly unacquainted not only with the

superfluous but the necessary Conveniences so much sought
after in Europe, they are happy in not knowing the use of
them. They live in a Tranquillity which is not disturbed by
the Inequality of Condition: the Earth and sea of their own
accord furnishes them with all things necessary for life.

Later, as other options declined and missionaries gained more
power over their charges, farming was established on the mission settlements. Outside the missions, men of mixed blood of
the second and later generations took up farming and sometimes
asked unsuccessfully to benefit from the schemes to settle small-
holders on the land. But Aborigines living in a traditional way
still do not take to farming and will get out of it if they can. In
the north, when the missionaries and government officials left
in the 1970s, the gardens fell into ruin. An anthropologist studying the people at an old mission on Cape York in the 1970s found
that the only people interested in keeping the gardens going
were outsiders, Melanesians and Torres Strait Islanders. The
Aborigines said, 'It is not our way; it is alright for other people.'

The British in Australia who wanted Aborigines to 'progress' by becoming farmers themselves 'regressed'. The best
way of making money turned out not to be agriculture but
herding. The country was not covered with fields of grain but
with sheep and cattle, which grazed on what had been the
Aboriginal hunting grounds.

After the frontier violence was over on the mainland (it
was different in Tasmania), the Aborigines remained on or near

their traditional lands. Their numbers were much reduced, though more by disease than violence. It was only much later that their movements were controlled and they were forced to move to missions or settlements and remain there. In a sparsely settled country with no fences and no made roads, there were plenty of places for them to camp and mind their own business. The pastoralist who had fought them for their lands now looked to employ them. The Aborigines were much more willing to become herders than farmers. They had a deep empathy with animals; they quickly learnt their habits, treated them carefully and could track them when they had to be rounded up. For cattle work the stockmen were mounted, and the Aborigines became expert horseriders.

In the better lands closer to the coast, only one or two Aborigines might be employed because European workers were available. When they were in short supply during the 1850s gold rushes, pastoralists were forced to rely much more on Aborigines to shepherd their sheep and found them to be much better workers than they expected. The more remote the pastoral station, the greater was the reliance on the Aborigines. Across the north of the continent they composed the whole workforce. The pastoralists were not concerned to civilise or Christianise their Aboriginal workers. A Wiradjuri man told the missionary at Wellington Valley, in New South Wales, why he was not returning to his ministrations: 'What for you speak much about God, and devil, and dying? No other white fellow, no other master, talk that way.'

The Aborigines who took work did not want to work regularly; they would work and then wander off with their own people or over their own country, taking work elsewhere or scrounging or hunting. In the north, where pastoralists were absolutely reliant on the Aborigines, they had to use force twice: first to claim the land, and then to grab and keep a workforce. A compromise was reached: in the wet season the Aborigines left the station and went 'walkabout' with their own people and on their own land.

Not all the Aborigines worked. On a Northern Territory station the young men and women worked, while the children and the old people lived in a camp a little distance from the homestead; out in the bush were the *myall*, or 'wild', Aborigines who had not come in to live and work on the stations. The workers were fed and clothed by the boss; the camp Aborigines were fed; the wild blacks still hunted and sometimes killed cattle.

Across all three groups traditional life continued. Marriages were arranged in the proper way, young men were initiated, corroborees were held. Working for the boss was understood in a traditional way. The workers were not getting a wage and they did not look to receive one; they were doing the work for this strong man, who in return would support and protect the whole community. It was a reciprocal relationship, as was common between kin, and bosses were sometimes treated as kin. The Aborigines were proud of their skills with the cattle, which they expressed in an organic way: 'We were born in the cattle;' 'We grew up the stations.'

This regime came to an end in the 1960s, when the pastoralists were told that the small wage that they were paying by this time had to be raised to the white worker's level. They then ceased to employ Aborigines and support the Aboriginal camps. The Aborigines became dependent on welfare.

New prospects beckoned soon after: those Aborigines with traditional connections to the land could become its owners under the land rights act passed by the Commonwealth government for its Northern Territory in 1976 (preceding the High Court's ruling in *Mabo* by sixteen years). There was now the opportunity for Aborigines to run their own cattle stations.

These have been tried but without much success. Europeans run cattle stations to make money, but this is not a preoccupation of Aborigines. Their clan and family loyalties undermine the efficient running of a business. Aborigines in these remote areas remain dependent on welfare, which troubles them less than those who want them to live to the standard of the rest of the community, to be healthy, well educated and employed.

The mindset of the hunter-gatherers survives.

HOW DID A PENAL COLONY CHANGE PEACEFULLY TO A DEMOCRACY?

THE PENAL COLONY OF NEW SOUTH WALES, established in 1788, became by 1860 a self-governing colony and a democracy, with all men having the right to vote. How did this amazing transformation happen? Some books do not pose this question at all; others give a variety of unconvincing answers, which mark the change rather than explain it.

The vagueness and thinness of the answers arise because the question has been wrongly posed. New South Wales did not begin as a penal colony; it is better to think of it beginning as a colony of convicts. Its history can be represented in this way:

Why wasn't early New South Wales a penal colony? The short answer is that British officials in 1786 could not conceive of such a beast: a society of warders and prisoners designed for punishment and control, as the French ran much later on Devil's Island. In Britain in the eighteenth century there was no institutional treatment of convicted criminals; they were flogged or hanged or sent to the American colonies.

There were gaols but only for short-term imprisonment. They were prisons without prison discipline. There was a men's ward and a women's ward, and no bar to the men and women intermixing. One convict couple who came on the First Fleet had met and conceived a child in gaol. If you were a prisoner of some means you could send out for food and other comforts, and maybe pay the gaoler in order to occupy a room in his house. Running an institution without reference to the birth, wealth and connections of the inmates was unimaginable.

We can understand the mindset of the ministers and officials who established New South Wales by looking at what they planned when the convicts were to be sent to the west coast of Africa (a plan that was abandoned because the climate was too hostile).

The convicts were to be dumped on an island in the Gambia River and left to their own devices. They were to elect a chief and a council to make laws and administer the settlement. It was to be a little republic of convicts. They were to cultivate the ground to support themselves; at this, some would undoubtedly do better than others, and they would become employers of the rest. The British government would keep a ship at the mouth of the river to see that they did not escape. Clearly, ministers were not concerned to punish these men according to their crimes; the punishment was to be exile. The men most likely to emerge on top in this little republic would be the most hardened and enterprising offenders.

With New South Wales, the government was much more involved: there was a governor and a contingent of marines. But quite quickly this new settlement began to look something like a republic of convicts. On day one the marines went on strike: they refused to supervise the work of the convicts. They refused to supervise the convicts even when they were clearing the ground for the marines' own tents. So Governor Phillip was forced to appoint convicts to oversee the work of other convicts. Their pay was the freedom not to work. The official rule was that convicts were to work from dawn to dusk, but the convict overseers soon adopted their own system to get work out of convicts. They fixed a daily task—so many trees felled; so much ground hoed—and when that was done the convicts were free to leave. If the convicts applied themselves, their task could be finished by midday.

This is how the convicts developed what they called their 'own time', which they defended ferociously. If the weather was bad in the morning and the government task could not be done, they refused to work for the government in the afternoon. In their 'own time' the convicts could laze about, steal, or take work and get paid for it.

It took years for governors to claim back at least some of the afternoon. The final rule was that the convicts had to stay at work either for the government or their private master until three o'clock. Governor Macquarie in 1814 declared that convicts had to work the full day for their private masters, but the masters had to pay for the work they did after three o'clock. This became known as their wage. For the convicts who worked for the government in Sydney, Macquarie built a barracks, which still stands in Macquarie Street. Once they had full board and lodging, the convicts did not need to earn money after three p.m. to pay for their private lodgings. But the convicts' 'own time' was not forgotten; at weekends they were free to leave the barracks and live it up or work in the town.

In the second year at Sydney Cove, food supplies were shrinking and starvation loomed. Desperate to stop robberies, Phillip created a police force and had no choice but to staff it with convicts. These convicted felons were given authority over free men, the sailors and the marines; in particular, they were to detain any marines or sailors who were wandering around the camp at night.

Under these orders, the convict police did detain marines, but after several months the head of the military (and lieutenant governor), Major Robert Ross, raised a furious objection when a marine was detained. Phillip had trouble eliciting his reasons; he was almost apoplectic with rage and could only repeat that the power given to the convict police was an insult to his corps. Which, by all ordinary standards, it was. Phillip yielded so far as to alter the rules for the police so that they could detain marines only if they were actually committing a robbery. Then he sent Major Ross to take charge at Norfolk Island. The convict police remained.

Convict overseers and police: this was just the beginning. For all professional services, the governors drew on the convicts: lawyers, architects, surveyors, doctors, teachers, artists (who were former forgers). It was hard to get free people to come to the colony to do these tasks. The second governor, John Hunter, told the British government to stop looking for eligible free people; whatever he wanted doing, there was a convict who could do it. Free settlers also employed these convict professionals; a convict tutor was a regular feature of a gentleman's home.

This so-called penal colony was run according to the principles of the ordinary English law. This was a late decision in the planning of the colony, taken, it seems, by Lord Sydney, the British home secretary, which is enough to warrant the immortality he has acquired through the city that bears his name. The first plan was for the colony to be governed under military law. The operation of the normal law meant that convicts could not receive any further punishment except by order of a court, and that before the court they appeared in the usual way, as innocents until proven guilty.

In fact, it became inadmissible to refer to a convict in court as a convict or ex-convict. In the magistrates' court, where convicts were taken by their masters for offences against the labour code—being lazy, running away, getting drunk—they were unlikely to get off, though it was a great access to their dignity that their masters could not punish them themselves. Convicts did not work under the lash. For serious offences in the higher courts, the rate of acquittal was quite high—between a quarter and a third of all cases. The juries in these trials were six military or naval officers, who were partial when cases touching on their honour and interests arose, but otherwise were conscientious and willing to let a convict or ex-convict go free if the evidence against them was insufficient.

Convicts acquired more legal rights in the colony than they had at home. Convicts in England could not give evidence, own property or bring actions in court. Since in New South Wales most people were convicts, they had to be allowed to give evidence if the court was to learn what it needed to know about a case. Because convicts could testify, they could give evidence against their masters. Convicts also had to be considered as owners of property, otherwise other convicts could not be charged with pinching it. The first case in the criminal court concerned a convict who had stolen another convict's bread ration.

If convicts were to protect their property, they had to be able to bring actions in court. The first case in the civil court was brought by a convict couple against the captain of the ship that had brought them to the colony. These were the convicts who had met in gaol, Henry Kable and Susannah Holmes. The government had at first planned to separate them, sending only Susannah and her baby to the colony. When the gaoler delivered Susannah and the baby to the ship, the captain refused to take the baby. The gaoler left Susannah at the ship and took the baby to London, where he camped outside the offices of Lord Sydney until he agreed that the baby and its mother and father could go to the new colony together. The case became famous and a fund was opened to equip the family for their new life. This was the baggage that the captain of the ship lost as they sailed to Australia. The court ruled that the captain had to pay the couple compensation.

The early governors were given no instructions as to the punishment of the convicts. The first job of the governors was survival; the second was economic growth, so that the colony could pay for itself. So they used the convicts according to their skills and diligence. They readily granted pardons to those who did good service, as well as to those who brought recommendations from home. The 'ticket of leave', which became a reward for good behaviour, was at first given to convicts who could get their own living and so be taken off the ration rolls. That reduced expenditure, which was what the British government was most concerned with.

Convicts had in this free-wheeling outfit plenty of opportunity to make money. The convicts who did best worked for the officers who had gone into the business of trading. Like all officers, they offset the tedium of a foreign posting by enriching themselves. They could import rum, tea, sugar and tobacco, but they could not actually set up a shop to sell them without damaging their claim to be gentlemen. The convict servants assigned to them ran the shops, and quite soon set themselves up in business on their own account, becoming traders, shipbuilders and bankers. These ex-convict businesspeople—men and women—were assigned convicts to work for them on the same terms as the officers and the few free settlers.

On becoming free, convicts were granted thirty acres as a farm and convict servants to help them work it. Few of the convicts were experienced or determined farmers. Most drank too much, fell into debt and sold off their lands, which were then bought by the more enterprising settlers, whether free or ex-convict. Some ex-convicts became wealthy landowners, but the route to this was in the first place through trade; starting with thirty acres was not the way fortunes were made.

Only one barrier was erected against the successful ex-convicts: no matter how much money they made, the officers and free settlers would not accept them as social equals. They did not expect to meet them at balls and dinners at Government House, which set the standards of 'good society'. To modern Australians this seems snobbishness, but the other side of this social exclusion was economic opportunity: the officers

and free settlers did not care what positions ex-convicts held
or how much money they made because they would remain
socially their inferiors.

Governor Macquarie thought the free settlers were
always bitching, and that it was the ex-convicts who had made
the place. He 'went native' and, fully accepting the logic of a
convict republic, appointed three ex-convicts as magistrates;
he invited them to Government House and expected the rest of
the Government House crowd to accept them as equals. They
deeply resented this, and this was one complaint that led to an
official enquiry into the running of the colony. Macquarie was
to be the last ruler of a colony of convicts.

But what about the floggings? This is what everyone
knows about early New South Wales. There was a good deal of
it. It was a regular punishment of the time used in the armed
forces, the schools and the home. It is so obnoxious to us that
it fosters misleading views of how the colony operated. When a
flogging is depicted in film or on TV, a cruel, sneering free settler sends his convict off to the court for a trifling offence. The
magistrate, who is a friend of the master, takes little time to
convict him. The order of the court is that the man be flogged.
There is a rattle of a drum; a small contingent of soldiers leads
the culprit forth; an officer gives an order; the culprit is tied to
the triangle; a soldier wields the whip.

This is entirely fanciful. The military had nothing to do
with convict punishments. A convict or ex-convict policeman
supervised the floggings, which were performed by a convict

flogger. The convict could as well be sent for punishment by an ex-convict master. During the Macquarie madness, the magistrate might have been an ex-convict. That's the picture to hold on to: an ex-convict master sends his convict to court; he is tried by an ex-convict magistrate; his punishment is supervised by an ex-convict policeman and he is flogged by a convict. Is this a penal colony? No, it's a unique social formation.

New South Wales was entirely different from the penal settlements, properly called, that were established by the French in the 1850s in colonies that already existed, Guinea and New Caledonia. The warders and the prisoners were in a special separate settlement. The warders did their job—they kept the convicts to hard labour—and the convicts and their skills were not called on to secure survival. The settlements were all-male affairs. They did not have a transforming effect on the colonies in which they were placed.

It was, finally, the presence of women in New South Wales that makes 'penal colony' so inappropriate a term. The rulers of Britain were happy to hang and flog prisoners but they thought locking men away from female company for a long period was unnatural and cruel. So 191 women convicts were sent on the First Fleet to accompany the 568 men. Governor Phillip planned to bring other women from the Pacific islands to service the men, but once he arrived he decided that it would be unkind to bring them to a colony close to starvation.

Men and women together: this was a source of much disorder—and also of babies. There were babies conceived on the

First Fleet. These infants were free British subjects. So before it began, this 'penal colony' was producing free people who grew up to call it home and thought of it as a nation in the making. Not even in its first year was this society composed just of convicts and their guards. In any case, the guards, as we have seen, were non-players in the penal department.

*

New South Wales was founded just as the cause of prison reform was taking off in Britain. The reformers wanted prisons to be well run, clean and healthy; the prisoners were to be classified, with men and women separated; and they were to be kept at work and attention given to their reformation. Solitary confinement was to be provided as a mode of punishment and an encouragement to reflection and reformation. When the reformers triumphed in the 1840s, solitary confinement was to be the lot of all prisoners. This was the terrible end point of a movement that thought of itself as humane and whose supporters worked as well on the abolition of slavery.

As these principles of punishment were accepted, New South Wales became a blot on the system. Here there was no classification, an indiscriminate mixing of the convicts, and no matching of punishment to crime or attempt at reformation. How could there be reformation when the convicts themselves composed almost the whole of the population? How could transportation be a deterrent when convicts lived well and some made fortunes? The reformers wanted transportation to New South Wales to be abandoned and all prisoners confined to prisons of the new type.

Building prisons according to the new principles was very expensive; expelling convicts out of the country was cheaper and psychologically very satisfying. Governments would not readily give up transportation but they had to take notice of the new principles. To this end, the government sent a commissioner of enquiry, John Bigge, to New South Wales in 1819. His brief was to find a way to make New South Wales a fit place for punishment, both for deterrence and reformation. After eighteen months of enquiry he produced his recommendations, which the British government adopted and Governors Brisbane (1821–1825) and Darling (1825–1831) carried out. This was the second stage in the colony's history: the attempt to make it into a penal colony. How far was it successful?

In future, tickets of leave were to be given only to those who had been well behaved. Governor Macquarie had set rules so that convicts could not get a ticket until they had served a certain proportion of their sentence; seven-year men had to serve at least three years. But he had frequently broken his own rules, and the convicts, in their bolshie way, had come to assume they had a *right* to a ticket as soon as they had served the required time, no matter whether they had convictions for drunkenness or running away.

To ensure that each convict's record could be known, there were now to be central records kept of all offences committed.

This took some time to organise and the records were never per-fect. They were much better in Tasmania, where on one page in the 'Black Books' all the details of the convict's career were recorded. Most of the New South Wales records were destroyed; the Tasmanian records survive and are a wonderful resource for family historians.

So on this matter convicts were now handled in a bureau-cratic way, with like cases treated alike—the same mindset from which came the notion of the well-ordered prison. The new system was a benefit to the convict who had no outstand-ing skill and no one to speak for him; if he kept his head down and did his work, he would get his ticket. Exceptions still had to be made: tickets were given out to those who caught bush-rangers or gave useful information about the hard men and their plans, or agreed to go on an exploring expedition. And letters of recommendation from home could sometimes still get a result—an early ticket of leave. But the problem of what to do with gentlemen convicts was partly solved. A special set-tlement was created for them, but they were not to be put to ordinary labour; no one could contemplate that.

Convicts were no longer to receive a wage. But this did not mean that all convicts got their ration and nothing else. Skilled men would be given extra rations and the opportunity to do work in their own time and be paid for it, either by a master or a neighbouring settler. In 1833 the leader of one of the rare convict rebellions claimed in court that he and his fellow con-victs had been repeatedly flogged and starved on the property of James Mudie in the Hunter Valley. Governor Bourke ordered an enquiry, which showed that these claims were untrue. It revealed that the leader of the rebellion, John Poole, was a carpenter in charge of a group of convicts who were building a windmill on the property. He got extra rations, including wine, and wore a white shirt. Mudie brought him a flute and a music book from Sydney. He got extra work making ploughs for other settlers. He got on well with Mudie but not with his son-in-law, who managed the property. When the son-in-law sent him to be flogged for insolence (his first flogging), Poole organised the revolt.

The food ration for convicts had been set down in London. It had been cut down in starvation time, restored and varied, but it survived as a standard that had to be met. It became the convict's right to receive seven pounds of flour and seven pounds of meat per week. In 1823 this was abandoned and convicts were to receive what was 'adequate'. About this there were many disputes. Convicts up on a charge of being lazy would claim they were being starved, and magistrates would have the difficult job of working out whether the food they received was 'adequate'. Convicts thought anything other than white bread was definitely not adequate; they were not going to eat brown bread or maize meal. In 1831 the official ration was restored.

Regular and uniform discipline was now to operate in the places of secondary punishment. These were the settlements at Port Macquarie and Moreton Bay, where convicts who had committed serious offences in the colony were sent. They had been as lax as early New South Wales itself. The military ran their own farms and employed convicts on them. Friends of the convicts could send them food, clothing and other goods—free of carriage on the government supply boats—so convicts could run shops while they were being punished. Married convicts were allowed to have their wives and children join them, and they were allowed time off to work in their support. From the ranks of double-convicted prisoners, constables and overseers were recruited. Now private farming and business were banned; all convicts had to be kept at hard work, with the hoe, not the plough, except that skilled men could work at their trades in cases of urgency—but only as a temporary measure. Well-behaved men could still have their wives join them. The overseers remained the convicts themselves.

In 1825 Norfolk Island was reopened. It had been an important adjunct to the early colony because it was so fertile, but it had not been used as a place of further punishment. Now it was to be a dreaded place of secondary punishment, the horror to keep men in order in New South Wales proper. Governor Darling ordered that no women were to be allowed, either wives of convicts or of soldiers. He acknowledged that the absence of women would lead to an increase in homosexuality, but he thought that the presence of a few women would not make much difference to its prevalence. In any case, his aim was deterrence; he didn't mind how bad a place he created. Whether he was right about homosexuality or not, Darling correctly gauged the significance of barring women.

He did not want the regularity of his prison disturbed by the comforting regularities of family life, or by the irregularities of the casual congress between men and women which had been part of life in every other settlement in New South Wales. Norfolk Island came closest to being a penal settlement, and could be so described if the convicts themselves were not the warders. Hated by the men as traitors and fearing always for the security of their jobs, they were the more tyrannical and cruel.

At Norfolk Island and at Port Arthur, in Tasmania, another place of secondary punishment, there are ruins of prisons built on the new principles of solitary confinement. At Port Arthur a wing of the separate prison has been restored, which includes the chapel where prisoners were seated in winged stalls to prevent them from seeing one another—so that solitary confinement would continue even in church. These relics are taken to be symbols of the convict system in Australia and its studied cruelty. They were actually built very late, to the formula of the British penal reformers who opposed transportation to Australia and the customary treatment of the convicts there. What was normal in the convict system has left no distinctive relics because most convicts saw out their time working for private masters, living in attics or separate kitchens, in the men's huts at a sheep station or in a shepherd's hut in the bush, or sharing bed and board with a small farmer.

That was the difficulty of running New South Wales proper according to penal principles. Private employers would never be concerned with punishment and reformation. They wanted to get work done, and they would cut deals and turn a blind eye as required. Bigge's plan to forestall this criticism was that more free settlers should be encouraged to come to the colony. They would make better masters for convicts than the ex-convicts. If all convicts were sent to do hard work on their estates in the country, there would be consistency in punishment and more chance of reformation away from the fleshpots of Sydney. It was a neat solution but this part of Bigge's report could not easily be implemented.

Four years after Bigge's policy was adopted, the British colonial secretary told Governor Darling that there were still too many skilled convicts in Sydney. He wanted them sent to the country and put to hard labour. Darling explained that he could not obey this instruction: if he did, how would the various trades of Sydney—tailor, shoemaker, etc.—be carried on? The building workers were even more important; they worked for the government during the week and took private work at the weekend: 'Thus has the Town of Sydney been built.' These were very stubborn facts to be put against penal principles. Whitehall let the matter drop.

One further difficulty about arranging hard labour in the country was that, increasingly, the work was minding sheep (boring but not hard) or rounding up cattle (exciting, with the freedom of being mounted on horseback). As pastoralism spread beyond the boundaries, the men who owned the stock usually did not supervise the enterprise themselves. So convicts had overseers who were ex-convicts, ticket-of-leave men or even other convicts. This was not a recipe for good order and tight discipline. The perpetrators of the 1838 Myall Creek massacre, in which thirty Aborigines were slaughtered, were convict and ex-convict stockmen who had been roaming the district on horseback for days, looking for Aborigines to kill.

Better order could have been established over convicts, and better protection for the Aborigines provided, if the rush to new lands beyond the boundaries had been stopped. But the British government wanted the wool that the colony provided. A booming colonial economy trumped penal principles.

More free settlers with capital did arrive in the 1820s, and were allocated land and convicts to work it. The Hunter Valley, settled at this time, did develop as Bigge had wished. In other new areas some ex-convicts were among the pioneers, especially in cattle, which required less capital. Ex-convicts were strongest in trading, shops, pubs, farming and other small businesses. Overall, they employed about half of the convicts working for private masters. No one (not even Bigge) proposed that they should be deprived of their convict workers. To do so would have knocked out half the economy, something that would have damaged free settlers as well. Since ex-convicts were so well established so early, it would take a long time before the great majority of convicts had free settlers as masters.

A court ruling just before Bigge arrived in the colony had cast doubt on the legitimacy of the pardons the ex-convicts had received. If the pardons were doubtful, the next query might concern their capacity to hold property. Though Bigge doubted their quality as masters, he could see that the prosperity of the colony depended on the security of their property. He added his support to the petition already sent to Britain asking for the pardons to be validated by parliament. This was done in 1823. That gave the ex-convicts what the certificate of freedom (a local invention) had long claimed: that the holder was 'restored to all the rights and privileges of free subjects'.

Overall, the changes made to the convict system following Bigge's report fell a long way short of his plan for all the convicts to be working in the country under the supervision of respectable free settlers. That arrangement might warrant the title 'penal colony'; I call the efforts made after his report a failed attempt at a penal colony. Too much could not be undone or bent to penal purposes.

*

The danger to New South Wales evolving into a free and democratic society came from the free settlers. If they had had their way, they would have made themselves into a ruling class and excluded the ex-convicts from power. The British government, which kept firm control over the colony, was the force that prevented this.

Britain was the pioneer liberal state. In the seventeenth century, parliament had tamed the monarchy by beheading one King and exiling another. The King still ruled but only parliament could pass laws and approve taxes. The King appointed judges but only parliament could dismiss them, an arrangement that established the law's independence. That all Englishmen were entitled to the protection of the law, conducted without fear and favour, was a deeply entrenched belief. Only a few Englishmen voted, but all had the right to the security of their property and persons, and to be tried by a jury of their peers. This view was held strongly enough by Lord Sydney that he felt that the convicts in New South Wales should be subject to the rule of law and not to some arbitrary authority. They did miss out on having a jury of their peers.

The American Revolution of 1776 proclaimed liberal principles, and the French revolution of 1789 liberal and then democratic principles. Democracy made liberalism look dangerous, for the French people had used their new power to chop off the heads of aristocrats and support a reign of terror. While the French revolutionary regimes survived, the British government hounded democrats and refused to contemplate any further liberal reform. But after 1815, when Napoleon was defeated, liberalism strengthened in Britain, with its chief aim the widening of the ranks of those who could vote for parliament.

In 1830, after long years of Tory rule, the Whigs, the reforming party, came to power in Britain. In the first *Reform Bill* of 1832 they gave middle-class men the vote and rearranged electorates, taking members away from small and decaying towns and allotting them to the new industrial cities. To New South Wales they sent a liberal governor, Richard Bourke. The ministers concerned with this oddball colony took their responsibility very seriously. They were appalled at what their predecessors had done: establishing a society of convicts, which was bound to create a degraded and immoral society. The concern for morality was strengthening alongside support for liberalism. The assumption that a colony of convicts must be degraded overlooked all the ex-convicts who had acquired property and so become defenders of law and order. Still, there was enough crime and drunkenness in New South Wales to give moralists cause for concern.

Viscount Howick, the son of the Whig prime minister, Earl Grey, was the minister responsible for colonial policy. He introduced a scheme to encourage free working people to migrate to New South Wales. In the 1830s there were thus two streams of migration: convicts and free working people. The convicts were still nearly all men; the free workers were men and women in equal number, which would help to redress the sex imbalance, a prime cause of immorality and disorder.

Working people could not afford to pay for the long journey to Australia. Howick got the money for their fares by introducing the sale of the colony's crown land, rather than giving it away. This was the formula advanced by the colonial reformer Edward Gibbon Wakefield. The selling of land would stop settlement spreading too far, and with the proceeds spent on the emigration of free people the colonies would not have to depend on convicts for their labour force.

The free settlers of New South Wales had not requested such a scheme and were dismayed that the land, which had been available as a free grant from the crown, now had to be paid for. They were even more dismayed when the price of land was ramped up during the 1830s to match the price in South Australia, which had been founded on Wakefield principles without convicts in 1836. The landholders of New South Wales were perfectly happy to go on relying on convicts. But the Whig government had now provided a way for the colony to continue to prosper if transportation were ever to cease.

With the support of the Whig government, Governor Bourke set new principles of equality in the government's dealing with the churches. Bourke was an Irishman, a Protestant but a liberal Protestant who had seen firsthand the bitterness and conflict caused in Ireland by the British government enforcing support of a Protestant church. Though most of the Irish were Catholic, they had to pay church rates to support Protestant ministers whose services they did not attend. The Whig government was contemplating directing funds to the Catholic Church in Ireland, but it was tricky: there were Protestant dissenters in England who did not want to pay church rates to the established Church of England and would be eager to take changes in Ireland as a precedent. The Whigs had no wish to encourage debate about the funding of the Church of England in England.

New South Wales was easier; the government approved Bourke's plan to support the Anglican, Catholic and Presbyterian churches on the same basis: the government would pay the salaries of their clergymen and would match the monies they raised for church building. The Catholics had been not altogether excluded from government support in New South Wales but now, at a stroke, they were to gain full equality with the Protestants. It was an amazing measure for Protestant Britain to sanction for its convict colony, and vital for social peace when almost a third of the population was Catholic. The Anglican bishop and other Protestant leaders did not like the government supporting the 'error' of Roman Catholicism, but they were pleased to have the promise of more generous support for their own churches. No one denomination could have proposed that others should receive government support as well as itself. This was a measure which only a benevolent despot could propose.

The fight for religious equality was one of the great liberal and radical causes in Britain throughout the nineteenth century. This highly charged issue had been put to rest in New South Wales long before the colony began to govern itself.

Again with the support of the Whig government, Governor Bourke introduced juries of citizens to try criminal cases in the place of juries made up of military and naval officers. In the usual way, jurymen had to own or occupy property of a certain value in order to be eligible to serve. Despite the fierce objections of the free settlers, Bourke allowed ex-convicts who met the property test to serve. The free settlers had some reason for their objection: there was an oddity, to say no more, in inviting former criminals to determine guilt or innocence in criminal trials. In their eyes, that would threaten the integrity of the legal system and damage the reputation of the colony—and their own for living in it. But a larger question was at issue:

as the colony acquired the normal legal and political institutions, were the ex-convicts, a large and prosperous class, to be marked for exclusion? Bourke had given his answer.

If ex-convicts could serve on juries, what could be said against allowing them to vote? The battle over juries took place in a larger dispute over the future government of the colony. The British government was contemplating allowing New South Wales the traditional right of a colony to have an elected assembly that could pass local laws.

The demand for an assembly had been pushed by William Wentworth, who had the ambition to confer all the rights of self-government on his native land. He was the son of a convict mother. His father, well connected in the Irish aristocracy, had been three times charged with highway robbery but never convicted. He went into voluntary exile in New South Wales and became very rich. His son was sent home to be educated at Cambridge University. On his return in 1824, he started the first independent newspaper in the colony, *The Australian*, which agitated for a popular assembly. Wentworth would allow the ex-convicts to vote, and he proposed a property qualification so low that nearly all ex-convict men would qualify. They easily outnumbered the free settlers, so the colony would fall into their hands. This pleased Wentworth no end because he had been snubbed and humiliated by the free settlers.

Governor Darling had tried to curb *The Australian* and other independent papers but had been frustrated by a liberal chief justice, so that the press was freer in the convict colony than in Britain. Darling could not believe it: he had been sent to make New South Wales a credible place of punishment, and the ex-prisoners had their own newspaper to clamour for their rights and denounce him!

The free settlers were alarmed at Wentworth's campaign for an assembly and feared that the Whigs might be persuaded by it. They insisted that if there were to be an assembly, property rights alone could not be the qualification for the vote. Ex-convicts would have to show some sign of rehabilitation.

The Whigs came close to setting up an assembly but they worried and delayed. They did not want to impose some contentious test on ex-convicts as qualification for the vote, but nor did they want the colony to fall completely into their hands. Ministers solved the problem another way: they decided to abandon transportation. Once the flow of convicts stopped, the free settlers were less concerned about voting rights for ex-convicts, who would now constitute a declining proportion of the population. Free settlers and the native-born would soon outnumber them.

This is how it was managed. Transportation stopped in 1840, and in 1842 ex-convicts were allowed to vote and stand for a Legislative Council, two-thirds of whose members were elected and one-third nominated by the governor. This body would pass local laws, but the governor and his officials, appointed by the Colonial Office, still constituted the government. Full self-government had not been granted but the impasse over ex-convict rights had been solved.

The free settlers had not proposed the ending of transportation; nor had Wentworth and his ex-convict supporters. Both groups were appalled at the decision because it seemed to threaten the colony's prosperity and was accompanied by wholesale denunciations of the colony. The Whigs had abolished slavery in the empire in 1834, and now the case against slavery was extended to New South Wales. Society was said to be as debased there as in the West Indian slave colonies. It was not only that the convicts were not properly punished or reformed, but also that the masters had been corrupted by the absolute power they wielded over their 'slaves'. New South Wales was in fact very different from the slave societies: its 'slaves' had rights under the law, and many had former 'slaves' as their masters. But the passion now aroused by slavery was enough for the British government to make a decision, which created huge problems for itself: what to do with the convicts? Prisons of the new type would have to be built for them. Meanwhile, transportation was to continue to Van Diemen's Land, which got many more convicts than it could cope with.

New South Wales was set on the path to becoming a self-governing colony of free people. The convicts already arrived would serve out their terms or gain tickets of leave; ex-convicts had the same legal and political rights as the free settlers; the native-born, chiefly the children of convicts, had always been full British subjects. The need for more labour would be met by the migration of free working people. The process of becoming a colony of free people proceeded smoothly because of the decisions of the British government or its endorsement of what Governor Bourke proposed. In summary, these were the key measures:

- A scheme for the migration of free working people was introduced (which made it possible to stop transportation).
- The Catholic Church (whose members were overwhelmingly ex-convicts or convicts) was granted government funding on the same terms as the Protestant churches.
- Ex-convicts were allowed to serve on juries.
- A local assembly was not granted while ex-convicts and free settlers were in dispute over its composition.
- Transportation was abandoned, which allowed free settlers to accept that ex-convicts could vote and stand for the assembly.

It is a great record of statecraft, but this is not usually highlighted in histories of Australia: who wants to acknowledge that Australia owes so much to the Poms?

Britain was becoming a more liberal society during Australia's early years but was itself still far from democratic. Amazingly, the British, having laid the foundations for a liberal state in New South Wales, helped to ensure that it was democratic.

The qualifications for voting for the partly elected Legislative Council established in 1842 were set by the British government. It knew that property values were higher in the colony than in England, so the English qualifications would not be appropriate. In England the lowest qualification for the vote was the rental of a house at £10 per year. This gave the middle class the vote in the towns but not the working class. For New South Wales the rate was to be double that: £20 per year. Rents were so high in Sydney that this allowed some skilled workingmen the vote. Overall, though, the rent and property qualifications set for the colony had the same result as in England: only about one man in five had the vote.

With such a narrow electorate the members elected to the Legislative Council were the colony's elite: large landowners, squatters, merchants and professional men. One of the members elected in 1843 was Dr William Bland, an ex-convict who had been sentenced to transportation for killing his opponent in a duel. William Wentworth, the son of a convict mother, was the leader of the elected members who harassed the governor's officials (who were nominated members of the council) and demanded that the colony be granted full powers of self-government. Wentworth was putting his rabble-rousing past behind him. The free settlers were now willing to accept him as their political leader, though still not as their social equal.

In 1848 a small group of Sydney democrats—skilled workers and small traders—formed a reform association. They did not dare to demand votes for all men; they asked that the franchise for the Legislative Council be widened. They sent a petition to this effect to the British Colonial Office. The petition would have had no impact, except that it acquired a very effective advocate in London. This was Robert Lowe, a clever lawyer who had made his fortune in the colony and had returned to make his mark in England. He had won one of the seats for Sydney in the 1848 council election with the support of the democrats. He was no democrat himself, but in London he supported a wider franchise for the colony with an argument that could not be used in the colony. He said that under the existing rules, many ex-convicts qualified for the vote but the newly arrived free workingman did not. The usual rules did not apply (was not everything topsy-turvy in the convict colony?): you would get a more respectable electorate by *lowering* the qualifications.

It happened that a bill dealing with the government of the Australian colonies was passing through parliament as Lowe set up his scare about convict influence in the electorate of New South Wales. The bill provided that the system of a partly elected Legislative Council would be extended to South Australia, Tasmania and the new colony of Victoria, now to be separated from New South Wales. The voting qualifications in these colonies were to be the same as in New South Wales.

By the time this measure reached the House of Lords, Lowe's argument had prompted a moral panic about convict influence, and their lordships—for the first and last time in their history—made an electoral measure *more* radical: they halved the household qualification in the towns and gave the vote to small tenant farmers in the country. No one had asked for this in South Australia, Tasmania and Victoria; the group petitioning for it in Sydney was totally marginal. The House of Lords had given the democratic cause in Australia a great boost. Sydney's elite could not believe it. At the next election, in 1851, Wentworth told the newly enfranchised Sydney electors to their faces that they should not have been given the vote. He only just scraped back in as the third member for the city.

Just as these new qualifications came into operation, the gold rushes began. Property values soared and, as they did, more and more people qualified for the vote. With no change to the law, every householder in Sydney (and in Melbourne) qualified. Every hovel carried a rent of at least £10 per year. Household suffrage was only one step away from manhood suffrage.

In 1852 the British government finally announced that the Australian colonies (except Western Australia) could become self-governing. Each Legislative Council was invited to draw up a constitution for a parliament of two houses. Wentworth was in charge of this process in New South Wales, where the argument over constitution-making was most intense. In this colony, now over sixty years old, a well-established old order was determined to protect itself. Wentworth announced that he planned a 'British not a Yankee' constitution. To offset the influence of the workingman householders of Sydney, who already had the vote, he added to the electorate the respectable young men who were lodgers. It was a desperate ploy: he was staving off democracy by giving more people the vote!

Since Sydney and the other towns were the heartland of liberals and democrats, Wentworth allotted most electorates to the country. For the upper house he planned a colonial aristocracy to mimic the House of Lords. When that was laughed out of court, he substituted a nominated house to be chosen by the governor. He protected these two bulwarks against democracy—the imbalance of electorates and the nominated upper house—by providing that they could be altered only by a two-thirds vote in the parliament, a most un-British measure, borrowed from the United States' constitution.

The Australian constitution was sent to London to be enacted by the British parliament. The officials who checked it noticed that Wentworth had not provided for any general power of amendment. He had been so concerned to ensure that its key provisions could not be readily amended that he had not included any process for the amendment of its other provisions. The officials inserted a general power of amendment for *all* provisions by a simple majority. This meant that the two-thirds clauses could be repealed by a simple majority.

Wentworth was in London at the time, and protested at this gutting of his work. But he had a formidable antagonist in the secretary of state for colonies, Lord John Russell, who had been a Whig prime minister in the 1840s and the hero of the struggle to pass the *Reform Bill* in 1832. He wanted the colony to be free to reconsider any part of its constitution, so the new provision which undid Wentworth's two-thirds device stood.

The first ministry under self-government was conservative, but it promised to repeal the two-thirds clauses. How could this be resisted when the minister in London had so clearly endorsed it? With that barrier gone, a liberal government in 1858 was able to redress the great imbalance in the allocation of electorates. This was more crucial for the establishment of democracy than the adoption of manhood suffrage, which was also carried. That measure added far fewer men to the electoral roll than the changes made by the House of Lords, by property inflation and by Wentworth himself. It *disqualified* some men, because electors now had to have resided in the electorate for six months to get on the roll and in the colony for three years. The nominated upper house survived because it turned out to be more amenable to popular control than one elected on a narrow property franchise, which was what the other colonies had established. If the upper house of New South Wales was too obstructive, the government could recommend to the governor that new appointments be made.

It is sometimes said that Australian women did not have to struggle as hard to get the vote as their sisters in Britain and America. Australian women got the vote in the new Commonwealth in 1902 and in all the states by 1909. It was nevertheless a struggle from the time of the formation of the first women's suffrage league in 1884: a long series of meetings, deputations and petitions. Australian women had to stick at it much longer than the men; Australian men got the vote quickly and with almost no struggle at all.

WHY WAS AUSTRALIA SO PROSPEROUS SO EARLY?

I N THE 1870S AND 1880S AUSTRALIA HAD THE highest living standards in the world. The signs that it would afford a good living to ordinary people were evident very early in convict Sydney.

The colony of New South Wales was unusual on two grounds. It was a colony of convicts and a colony for which the British government took direct responsibility. Previously, colonies had begun as private ventures with governmental approval. If the colony failed or its pioneer settlers starved, that was of no concern to the British government. At Jamestown, the first English colony in North America, only sixty-one of the 500 pioneer settlers survived. When the British government sent convicts to the North American colonies, it took no responsibility for them. Contractors took them off its hands at the gaol gates.

When Lord Sydney saw the plans for the colony at Botany Bay, they provided for one year's supply of rations. He immediately doubled it to two years' supply. If this project was a disaster he would be in the firing line. Apart from men in the army and navy, the British government had assumed more direct responsibility for the convicts going to New Holland than for any other of His Majesty's subjects. The responsibility for success—or at least for avoiding failure—also weighed heavily on the first governor, Arthur Phillip. He took great pains to see that the ships of the First Fleet were well fitted out and carried all needful supplies, particularly medicines. He ensured the convicts had fresh food, including fruit and vegetables, until the ships sailed and at all ports on the way. At Rio boatloads of oranges came out to the convict ships and each convict got ten oranges, which would have helped to stave off scurvy. During the voyage, the convicts were allowed to exercise on deck. They remained remarkably healthy; only twenty-four died out of the 759 who sailed.

Despite the careful planning, the colony did come close to starvation. The land around Sydney was not suited to agriculture and the convicts were very unwilling farmers. They would not work well even though their lives depended on it—but in fact they didn't. Phillip could not let them starve. In October 1788, after the failure of the first harvest, he sent Captain John Hunter in the *Sirius* to Cape Town to buy flour and grain. Phillip recommended the shortest route to Hunter, west across the Indian Ocean. Hunter had other ideas: he sailed east, with the westerly winds always behind him, across the Pacific, around Cape Horn, across the South Atlantic, dodging the icebergs, to Cape Town, and then back to Sydney across the Indian Ocean. Hunter had circumnavigated the globe to keep the convicts alive. The tab for what he purchased at Cape Town was picked up by the British government.

ROUND THE WORLD TO FEED THE CONVICTS: CAPTAIN HUNTER'S VOYAGE

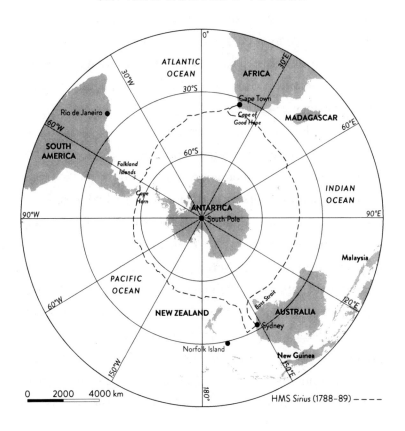

The plan for the colony was that the convicts would grow their own food on public farms. When their time was up, they would be given small plots of land, where they could grow enough to support themselves and their families. Had this plan been followed, the economic history of New South Wales would have mirrored that of Europe: for ages most people lived by subsistence, and trade and commerce played only a small part in the economy. The transition to a modern, dynamic economy depended on agriculture being drawn into the commercial world: farmers growing for a market rather than only for themselves, and becoming consumers of products made elsewhere. That transition was well advanced in Britain when New South Wales was founded; elsewhere in Europe the peasant world of self-sufficiency still survived.

When Phillip left Sydney in 1792, the colony was run for three years by the officers of the New South Wales Corps. They allocated farmland to themselves, shut down the public farms, moved the convict workers to their own lands, had the government store feed their workers, and sold the crops produced to the government store—which then distributed them to the convicts, including those working for the officers. The officer-farmers paid nothing for their land or their labour, and they had a guaranteed market for their produce! Not even the Russians after communism were so barefaced in transforming public goods into private profit. But the officers did manage to get more work out of the convicts. They were now growing enough food to feed themselves, but at great profit to the officers and at the expense of the British government, which had to cover the cost of what the store purchased. This was not subsistence farming, but commercial agriculture with a vengeance.

The government store paid for produce by bills on the British Treasury, pieces of paper that could be transferred into gold on presentation in London. Since the credit of the British government stood so high, these bills circulated as a sort of currency. The officers used them to operate as importers of goods either on their own account or by buying from captains and merchants who brought goods to the colony. These bills were Australia's first foreign exchange. The imports were goods of common consumption: tea, sugar, rum, tobacco. The officers either gave these to their own workers as inducements to work (particularly the rum) or sold them to convicts who paid for them with their extra earnings. Since the convicts got basic rations from the store, their extra earnings could be spent in this way. They entered the commercial world as consumers.

The convicts came not from a land of self-sufficient peasants, but from the most advanced commercial and industrial society on earth. As Grace Karskens reminds us, working people were drinkers of tea and ate from china plates rather than wooden bowls. The convicts were in a good position to demand that they live well. There was no one else to do the work. They insisted that the cereal portion of their ration be white bread. They did not want to eat maize or rye bread. Maize and rye grew better than wheat in some areas, but if a master wanted a contented workforce he had to buy in wheat. Australia was never a true pioneering society where people are obliged to eat what they can grow or collect. Maize cakes and maple syrup entered the diet of the American colonies. Australia's diet in its early years was white bread (or damper), tea, sugar and rum—with the tea, sugar and rum always imported, and sometimes the wheat. The consumption per head of all these items exceeded that in Britain. The convicts had more chance of regularly enjoying them than the lower orders at home.

The short answer to the question of why the standard of living was so high in convict Sydney is this: the officers who wanted to make a pile and the convicts who would work only for rum had contrived to make the British taxpayer support their lifestyle.

The sources of the colony's flourishing import trade were India and China. Living with Asia was the reality in 1800, not a slogan. By then, merchants from India were opening businesses in Sydney. A commercial centre in a so-called penal colony: there's a conundrum! (As we saw in Question 2, there are several other reasons for doubting the aptness of the term 'penal colony'.)

The British government was alert to the scam the officers were running at its expense. It wanted the officers to feed their convict servants and for public farming to be resumed. It took a long time to pull the officers into line, and public farming never again became the central institution of the economy. It was occasionally resumed—to employ surplus convicts or in pursuit of the chimera that it would be cheaper if convicts grew their own food.

The rule for convicts in private hands became that they should be fed by their masters according to the official ration. The store continued to feed the considerable number of convicts who worked for the government in administration and on public works, those in hospital and in gaol, and all the civil and military officers and their families. It fed and equipped new settlers on the land. It also brought in all the goods and equipment that a very active government required. The market the store offered was a key element in the colony's prosperity, and the Treasury bills it issued for its purchases continued for many years to be the chief source of foreign exchange. For the years 1788–1822, the economic historian Noel Butlin has estimated that British expenditure averaged two-thirds of the colony's gross domestic product.

The British government was always wanting the store's expenditure to be cut but it never got a handle on how the store was manipulated. There was outright fraud: the officer in charge of the store set up a biscuit-making business, with all the ingredients taken from the store and all the profits going to himself. It was standard practice for governors to pay for local administration not by taxing the inhabitants but by assigning to the office-holder one or more convicts fed by the store. The office-holder (it might be a constable or an overseer) did not need the convicts to do his job: he profited by renting the convicts out to others or by allowing them to work at some trade or business with the returns going to him. By this device, the subsidy to the colony from the British Treasury was increased.

The benefits that New South Wales had reaped by a steady stream of British spending were not lost on the pioneer colonists in Western Australia. Their colony, founded as a free settlement in 1829, languished; after twenty years the population was only 5000. Even when they found productive uses for the soil, landowners had difficulty in keeping labour. By asking for and receiving convicts in 1850, they gained the double benefit of cheap labour which could not decamp east, and British spending.

New South Wales would enjoy the British spending only while convicts continued to come. During the Napoleonic wars, the number of convicts sent dropped sharply (they were drafted into the army and navy instead), and Governor King (1800–1807) managed to follow his instructions and cut spending drastically. After the wars, from 1815, the convict flow started again, but for the moment Sydney's business world faced a crisis. If a replacement for Treasury bills as foreign exchange was not found, business would have to contract.

The saviour was the sealing industry, which provided skins and oil for export. Governor King gave his support to its development. The industry was not complicated: men were given rations and taken to the islands, where the seals would be clubbed to death. Boats were required, and so sealing provided a stimulus to shipbuilding in Sydney. For obvious reasons, convicts could not be sent on sealing expeditions; this was a business of free labour, chiefly ex-convicts.

The ex-convict merchants who got their start working for the officers were prominent in sealing. They were not going to be accepted as businesspeople outside New South Wales; they were shrewd, unscrupulous and desperate to succeed. James Underwood built ships for the sealing grounds, Henry Kable organised the sealing gangs, and Simeon Lord sold the oils and skins in London. These three former convicts kept the 'penal colony' in the commercial world and preserved its high standard of living.

When the seals had been clubbed almost to extinction, whaling became the chief earner of foreign exchange outside the store. Whaling began in the Southern Ocean just as New South Wales was founded. The first whalers were British and American; they used Sydney and Hobart as ports for replenishment and repair, which was good for local business, but their whale oil was not an Australian export. In the 1820s Australian merchants and traders joined in, and they had the advantage of having their base closer to the whaling grounds. Here distance was not a handicap, a point Geoffrey Blainey himself made in *The Tyranny of Distance*, which has an evocative chapter on sealing and whaling. Blainey was one of the first to point out that until the mid-1830s, it was this harvest from the sea rather than wool which was the chief earner of foreign exchange.

The boom in wool began in the 1820s. By 1850 all the good country in the south-eastern segment of the continent had been taken over by the sheep. The rougher country was given over to cattle. Grazing sheep was a highly efficient industry. Capital had to be invested in the sheep but in little else, and the beauty of this industry was that the capital reproduced itself: each year sheep had lambs. The grasslands were open because of the firestick farming of the Aborigines; no fencing was required; and buildings were of the simplest sort, wooden huts roofed with bark, whose use had been learnt from the Aborigines. Since the climate was mild sheep did not have to be under cover in the winter.

Flocks were at first penned at night around the shepherds' hut to protect them from dingoes. But these holding yards became messy, which caused damage to the fleece, and the grass around the yards was trampled down. So flocks then remained apart at night, penned behind temporary fences or hurdles out on the run. The watchman slept in an open box on legs, which could be carried from place to place.

Labour costs were kept down by increasing the number of sheep each shepherd had to watch. In the 1820s one shepherd cared for 300 to 350 sheep; by 1850 it was 1000. This risked more losses, and it may be that more convicts were flogged for losing sheep, though as settlement spread so rapidly, convicts were a long way from the courts and magistrates, which were needed if floggings were to be inflicted. Generally, the productivity of the economy in early New South Wales was higher because of the high proportion of single men of working age; the squatting districts were almost exclusively a male domain. Sheep did not have to support wives and children. There were Aboriginal women in the squatting districts whom the European males sought out for sexual release, consensual or otherwise.

Settlement could spread so far inland because wool was a light, highly valuable product, which could bear the cost of a long haul to the coast by bullock wagon. The trip around the world by sea to Britain was much less expensive. On their return journey from the ports the bullock wagons carried flour, tea, sugar and rum to feed and comfort the workforce. The great swathe of country behind the Great Dividing Range became part of the commercial world as soon as it was settled by Europeans. When the settlers in the United States moved westward over the Appalachians, they had to become self-sufficient farmers. They left the world of trade and wages for the security of owning their own land. Their isolation did not end until canals were built that connected them to the east and steamboats began operating on the river systems in the Midwest. That form of isolation is not part of the Australian story.

Economic growth in Australia did not require the incorporation of a backward, unproductive rural sector. When farming later developed on the pastoral runs, it was commercial farming. Australia, as its greatest historian Keith Hancock said, was born modern. The United States, by contrast, imitated to an extent the history of Europe. In areas which had been self-sufficient there was more regional variety in speech and habit. There were pockets of settlement which for a long time remained outside the commercial world, even when access to it became possible. Backwoodsmen, hillbillies and country music were the results.

Wool was not in itself the sole cause of the colony's growing prosperity. Because wool was booming, middle-class migrants left Britain, taking capital with them, English widows put their savings into Australian banks, merchants sent off imports on spec, and working people were lured by the prospect of high wages and meat three times a day. The government sold more land because of the expectation that land values would rise, and with the proceeds more working people were brought to the colony. James Belich has given us the term 'explosive colonisation' for this process.

Its most obvious effect in this period in Australia was the growth of Melbourne, the port for Port Phillip, then a squatting district of New South Wales. Founded in 1835, it had 23,000 people fifteen years later, an almost instant city. Port Phillip followed the Australian pattern: one-third of the population was in Melbourne, which was something more than a port for wool; it was an administrative, commercial and manufacturing centre. The building of the city itself provided much of the employment.

The open grasslands had been turned to good account, but a country can be resource-rich and still economic growth can stall. A resource may be locked away by its owners, to the detriment of everyone else. The men who grazed cattle on the Argentine pampas managed to make themselves owners of it, and so became a powerful force against democracy and economic development. Since Argentina had a similar resource base to Australia and yet ended up much poorer, it has regularly been used as a contrast to Australia.

The Australian squatters tried to lock their resource away and failed. At first they had no title to their lands (hence their name). In 1836 Governor Bourke, realising that the rush to new lands could not be stopped, legitimised it with an annual licence fee for squatting runs. The squatters wanted much more security than an annual licence; they claimed that, having transformed the wilderness, they should be granted the ownership of their lands. They ran campaigns in the colony and in London pushing their demands. In 1847 the British government relented and allowed them to have leases of fourteen years.

The squatters were satisfied, but this was not a complete victory. The tenure of their lands would be reassessed in fourteen years' time—which was exactly what Earl Grey, the British secretary of state for the colonies, wanted to ensure. He never thought colonial lands should be seized by the lucky first comers. As Viscount Howick, he had been responsible in 1831 for the new policy of selling land in Australia rather than giving it away. Nor did Earl Grey forget the original inhabitants of the grasslands: the leases for the pastoral runs included a clause that allowed Aborigines to continue to hunt over them. This did not give them much protection from the squatters, but in 1996 this provision in the original squatting leases was used by the High Court in *Wik* to declare that Aborigines had a continuing right over land under pastoral lease. Contrary to what was implied in *Mabo*, the first land rights ruling, a pastoral lease did not completely extinguish native title.

In 1851, just four years after the leases were promised, the gold rushes broke out. In Victoria where most of the diggers were at work, the good land around the goldfields was tied up in the squatters' hands. This was absolutely intolerable to men who wanted to buy land with their winnings, as an investment or to meet the food needs of the new gold towns. Governor La Trobe found a loophole in the leases: land could be withdrawn to make reserves for public purposes, such as townships and roads, 'or for otherwise facilitating the improvement and settlement of the colony'. Under this clause he took back thousands of acres from the squatters to create 'agriculture reserves', which were subdivided and sold off at auction. The squatters were furious and took their case to London. The Colonial Office backed the governor.

Gold, the great new resource, was open to all comers; anyone who paid a licence fee could dig. This was the system organised in Sydney in 1851 by Governor FitzRoy's chief official, the colonial secretary, Deas Thomson (not to be confused with the secretary of state for the colonies in London, to whom Thomson was responsible). This democratic treatment of the crown's resource was opposed by a number of the colony's large landowners, led by James Macarthur, the son of the wool pioneer. Their plan was that everyone should be kept out of the gold country until it was properly surveyed, at which time it would be leased out to private companies.

Thomson did not have the soldiers to drive off the diggers who were already at work, nor the inclination to do so. He drew up rules for taking out licences on small plots and sent an experienced local magistrate to institute the system. All went smoothly and the licence system for small claims was copied in Victoria. Here the fields were much larger and the heavy-handed administration of the licences led finally to revolt at the Eureka Stockade. As a result, the managing of the goldfields was passed to bodies elected by the diggers. They were very determined that gold-digging should stay open to the small man.

When news of the gold finds first reached Britain there was a rush to form companies to take up goldmining in Australia. Some of these were fraudulent; very few got as far as sending agents and managers to start work. They met a very hostile reception, especially in Victoria. They wanted portions of the goldfields allocated to them, which the Victorian governor refused to do, for fear of upsetting the diggers. These men and their principals had never seen the like: British capital being spurned in a British colony!

Because gold finding remained in the hands of the individual diggers, its benefits were quickly and widely spread. Goldfield earnings flowed directly into small business, farming and building, as well as into pubs and brothels. Farming in South Australia received a great boost, as farmers and their sons returned home from the diggings and bought up more land. Profits were not being exported out of the country. The finding of more gold was encouraged because the finder of a new field could immediately start working it.

Gold led truly to explosive colonisation. In ten years Victoria's population multiplied seven times, and Melbourne's five times. Melbourne eclipsed Sydney as the largest city in Australia, a position it maintained for forty years. Australia's population tripled from 400,000 to about 1.1 million. The economy expanded even more rapidly, with the result that the standard of living was higher at the end of the decade than at the beginning. For twenty years gold rather than wool was the chief earner of foreign exchange.

As the alluvial gold ran out, the diggers had reluctantly to accept that companies were needed to dig deeper shafts and pound the gold out of quartz. British capital had been scared away; the companies were small-scale and tied to one locality, with shares being bought not just by Melbourne investors but also by townspeople on the goldfields and the mineworkers themselves. British investment in mining became important at Charters Towers in Queensland in the 1880s and on the goldfields of Western Australia in the 1890s. The times were over when the Australian people laid hold of the precious metal and all the profits were theirs.

*

The decisions of the British government and its local officials had been firmly in the direction of keeping resources open, which led to a more dynamic economy. With the granting of self-government in the mid-1850s, liberal governments elected on manhood suffrage were determined to end the squatters' hold on the land. The term of the fourteen-year leases was expiring. 'Unlock the lands' was the popular cry. The first attempts to get small men onto the land, the *Selection Acts* of the early 1860s, were a dismal failure, always highlighted in the history books; their long-term success frequently goes unnoticed.

In Victoria, as we have seen, squatters' lands were already being sold for auction. This had led to a great growth in farming around the goldfields. But only men of some means could pay upfront the money for a farm. For men without the necessary funds, the governments now offered land on credit. The difficulty was that squatters could employ men to take up land on these terms, then transfer it to themselves. These were the 'dummies'. In Victoria great stretches of good land in the Western District passed back into the squatters' hands through the use of dummies. The new *Land Acts* had simply made lessees of land into its owners. But the land reformers persisted, and in time policies were developed to keep the squatters out. The moves made in New South Wales and Victoria are summarised in the following table.

THE MEASURES THAT MADE
THE *SELECTION* ACTS WORK

1. The abolition or limitation of open sales at auction. The *Selection Acts* had been designed because small men could not hope to compete against the pastoralists or speculators at auction sales, but liberal and democratic governments continued the auctions because they were an easy way of raising money.

2. Dummying—that is, the employment by squatters of men who selected on their behalf—was made more difficult by the

insistence that a selector could not obtain title to the land unless he had resided on it and improved it over a considerable number of years. The early Victorian legislation had allowed a selector to obtain title immediately if he had the funds. That meant a dummy only had to be employed by the squatter for a few days. He'd select the land, pay for it, then transfer it to the squatter. It was a much riskier and expensive business for the squatter if his dummy had to be employed for years before the title could be obtained.

3. The terms of repayment for the selector were made more generous, and eventually a system of leasing at low rental was introduced. This meant that the selector could afford to take up more land and could spend more of his capital on improvements and machinery.

4. More effective and flexible administrative procedures were developed. Land boards were set up to examine all applications for land. This helped screen out dummies and reduce the squatters' influence in the local administration of the law. Ministers of lands gained more power. They could cancel selections if they considered they were not bona fide. This proved much more effective than taking offenders through the courts.

When all this was accomplished, governments began to tax the large landed estates that had been accumulated in the early days of the *Selection Acts*, and then to buy them back and subdivide them into farms. The end result was that by the time of the First World War, a great wheat belt of family farms stretched across Victoria north of the Divide, and into New South Wales along the Divide's western slopes and out into the plains. South Australia had been a wheat-growing colony from the start; Victoria outstripped it in wheat production by 1881, New South Wales by 1897. This was a highly efficient commercial farming, with the crops being harvested by machinery. A great swathe of territory had been made more productive, and it supported many more people than the grazing of sheep. Democratic power had finally produced a change in the pattern of land ownership. Actually, sheep were still grazed but now on the stubble of the wheat paddocks as part of a mixed farming regime.

Wheat-growing only became possible beyond the Divide when the railways arrived. Wheat is a 'heavy' product and could not be carted far by bullock wagon before its value was consumed. If the squatters had been left in control of the land, they would have been the beneficiaries of the new opportunities for wheat farming. They would have rented out their lands to tenant farmers—as the owners of the pampas did in Argentina when the railways arrived. Would this have made any difference to economic growth? Yes; owners of family farms were better consumers and better able to protect and advance farming in democratic politics than poor tenants.

The railways were built and operated by the colonial governments. They were the biggest item in their programme of public works, for which they borrowed heavily in London from the 1850s onwards. Here was a trap. If this investment was not put to productive use, the economy would be held back. The signs did not look good. Party allegiance was weak in the colonial parliaments;

every member was angling to get money spent in his electorate and would offer and withdraw support to ministries accordingly. There was, unsurprisingly, a rapid turnover of ministries.

Governments and parliaments did assess the likely returns from railways before approving them. There was some uncertainty about the tests. Did government railways have to make a profit or just pay their way? Or could losses be borne because of the general benefits which improved transport brought? All these standards were used at the time, with a tendency to move towards the last. Latter-day economists adopt differing standards and come to different answers about the productivity gains of these investments. One wonders sometimes how much of private and public investment in colonial times would pass the tests of modern-day economists. As Belich reminds us, colonial booms were followed by colonial busts. Explosive colonialism was driven by a dynamic of high, even crazy expectations and not by cost-benefit analysis.

With colonial railway building, we are not examining a situation in which some of the loan money went into ministers' pockets, or lines to which money was allocated never got built or were built with substandard materials, with contractors pocketing the difference. Or where the system never turned a profit. In each colony there was remarkable continuity of service in the engineers who had charge of the railways. They were better known than the succession of ministers; they had their own overall plans for railway development and were quite capable of staring down the politicians.

The engineers in New South Wales and Victoria might be said to have been too powerful, for they insisted on building lines to the highest British standards—against the wishes of politicians, who wanted to build more rapidly light, narrow-gauge lines. These could bear tighter corners and hence required less earthworks. The engineer in Queensland was a narrow-gauge man, to the great benefit of that colony, which had fewer resources and more ports to link to their hinterlands. South Australia switched to narrow gauge to service ports on its two gulfs, and then joined them in a single network with the older lines around Adelaide (though with breaks of gauge). In New South Wales and Victoria it was only after trunk routes were finished that logrolling for branch lines set in. This was occurring in the smallest and richest colony of Victoria by the 1880s, but that was atypical of railway building in the previous thirty years. Overall, there was more coherence to the pattern of railway building than would be predicted from the chaos of personal and factional manoeuvring in the parliaments.

The governor appointed from Britain was the guarantor of the probity of Australian governments. Before self-government, governors were the actual heads of administration, and were in charge of the British officials who administered the various departments. With self-government, premiers and cabinet ministers responsible to parliament appeared, but governors did not disappear as active agents in administration. They were far from being figureheads. All important appointments and the approval of expenditure passed through the Executive Council, a meeting of ministers chaired by the governor. Governors also queried ministers and officials if they were concerned about some fault in administration.

Just how active governors were has now been made plain by a composite biography of *The Governors of New South Wales 1788–2010*. In 1904 a premier about to retire recommended the names of two men from his party who might succeed him. Governor Rawson refused to 'send for' either of them. One was unreliable and the other a drunk.

Perhaps it was in New South Wales that administration most needed the attention of a governor. But all the colonial parliaments were rough-houses compared with Westminster, and ministers were often inexperienced. The British governor and the Colonial Office to which he reported kept them under scrutiny.

The spending of large sums of borrowed money on 'developing the resources of the colony' was the consensus policy of colonial politics. Business liked the stimulus it brought and the benefits it promised; farmers and country towns wanted railways; small contractors, often farmers, got jobs on public works in their locality; workingmen got work. Because workingmen also had votes, they were able to pressure governments into being pace-setters on pay and conditions. Railways, water supply, ports and harbours: these were the biggest enterprises in colonial society, all run by the government. A victory here on pay and conditions was of great significance.

There was a division in colonial politics over the amount to be spent on immigration. Because Australia was so far from

Britain, migration to the United States and Canada was much cheaper. Immigration to Australia would be substantial only if governments subsidised passages. Farmers and business complained of scarcity or the high cost of labour and wanted more spent on immigration. Workers wanted immigration restricted or, better still, stopped so that the labour market would not be flooded. Candidates in working-class constituencies had to be anti-migration.

When Britain ran the colonies, half what it collected by land sales was devoted to immigration. With self-government, the colonies gained control over land and the proceeds of its sale. For governments the temptation to spend the proceeds of land sales on the ordinary business of government was very strong. They were selling off a capital asset but while sales held up taxation could be kept low. For their own reasons, then, governments were inclined to the workers' view of immigration. Queensland, less well developed and with smaller concentrations of workers in cities, was the only colony to retain a substantial immigration programme. Victoria and South Australia stopped theirs altogether. By their political pressure, workers ensured that Australia did not follow the United States, where immigrants flooded into the eastern seaboard cities and worked for low wages.

The years from the gold rushes of the 1850s to 1890 were almost universally prosperous. The pastoral industry continued to grow. It was being eased out in the wheat belt, but it was still the chief primary industry in the country overall. Its productivity improved still further by investment in fences, which removed the need for shepherds, and in dams, which increased carrying capacity. From 1870 wool was again the chief export, followed by gold and the newcomer, wheat.

It was in this period that Australia's standard of living overtook that of Britain and became the highest in the world. The measure for standard of living is rather crude: gross domestic product per head. That does not indicate how income is distributed within a society, or how standards differ across society. Fortunately, there are other measures that allow us to say confidently that Australian workers at that time had the highest living standards in the world, achieved in part, as we have seen, by political pressure brought by the workers themselves.

The workers had an annual festival to celebrate the good life they had achieved. This was Eight Hours Day. In 1856 building workers in Sydney and Melbourne, by concerted action and some brief strikes, acquired the eight-hour day—the first workers in the world to enjoy it. It was easy for building contractors to give in to this demand because buildings did not face competition from imports. Other tradesmen and unskilled workers had to work harder and wait longer to achieve the eight-hour day. Each year that first victory was celebrated by the trade unions, whose members paraded through the streets with their great banners. The parade was both a celebration of the eight-hour principle—eight hours' work; eight hours' recreation; eight hours' rest—and a demand that all workers should enjoy it. The day was a public holiday, and crowds gathered in the streets to watch the parade. The whole community took pleasure in Australia providing a better life for workingmen.

*

The 1880s was the last decade of prosperity. From around 1890 the economy crashed into depression, which was made worse by a long drought—known as the Federation Drought—that began in 1895. Australia never again enjoyed the highest living standards in the world. The events of this collapse and the responses to them set the course of public policy for almost a hundred years. How the new public policy affected the operation of the economy is a matter of dispute.

In the 1880s a new spirit moved among working people. Previously, trade unions had been small bodies limited to skilled workers and one locality; now the number of unions rose rapidly, they extended to semi-skilled and unskilled workers, and they included workers across the colonial boundaries. There were many strikes, most short-lived and successful. Unionists supported one another other in their struggles through formal organisations like trades and labour councils, by black bans on goods produced by non-unionists, and by direct giving. A new bond had grown among workingmen when seamen in Port Adelaide were agreeing to send money docked from their pay to striking bootmakers in Melbourne.

The rise in unions and labour organisations was a world-wide phenomenon in the 1880s: it happened in the United States, Britain and in western Europe as well as in Australia. This was a movement like that for female liberation and black emancipation in the 1960s. It was inspired by the hope that the exploitation of workers by bosses would disappear and be replaced by some form of socialist society. Workers knew they were joining a worldwide movement and gained strength and confidence from it. In 1889 donations from Australia enabled the dockworkers of London to win a strike for more pay.

In Australia by 1890, the rate of union membership in the workforce had become the highest in the world. Was this because pay and conditions in Australia were the worst? No; it was because they were the best. Workers who lived in a society that had already yielded so much to them were confident that it could yield much more.

In 1890 these hopes came crashing down. The unions blundered into a maritime strike that expanded into something close to a general strike. It spread from coastal shipping to the wharves, to road transport, coalmines and shearing sheds; with coal in short supply, railways and gas lighting of the streets were also affected. The employers were determined to win since unions were now demanding the right to insist on a 'closed shop'—the principle that all workers had to belong to a union. The employers refused to negotiate with the men; they recruited non-union labour, which was protected by police, and after ten weeks the unions were forced to capitulate. Governments had proclaimed they were neutral in this great battle, but to unionists the use of police to protect non-union labour made them partisan. It was the governments' siding with bosses that enraged the unionists most amid the humiliation of defeat. This was not a new world after all.

The response of the unionists was to push on more firmly their plans to form their own political party so that this could never happen again. In New South Wales the Labor Party was astoundingly successful on its first outing in 1891: it won a quarter of the seats and held the balance of power between free-traders and protectionists.

Many middle-class people were disturbed by the disruption and bitterness brought on by the strike. They might not have sympathised fully with the unions but they did not like the way they had been put down. These impulses strengthened the more progressive liberals in colonial politics, whether free-traders or protectionists. They developed schemes of compulsory arbitration to settle industrial disputes so that society would never again be paralysed by strikes.

The progressive liberals with Labor support were the predominant force in late colonial politics and in the new Commonwealth after 1901. Though Labor had misgivings about compulsory arbitration, it signed up to it. The unions had lost out badly on the ground in the 1890s. Defeat in 1890 had been followed by defeat in two shearing strikes in 1891 and 1894, and at Broken Hill in 1892. State-supported arbitration might bring results that they could no longer achieve for themselves. The Commonwealth Arbitration Court was set up in 1904. It did not manage to stop strikes, but its awards became the way that wages and conditions for an industry—in the most minute detail—were set for the whole country.

The Labor Party grew rapidly in the early Commonwealth. Its central concern was the improvement of workers' wages and conditions. On the issue that divided the other two parties—free trade or protection—it was neutral. When Alfred Deakin, the protectionist leader, made the protection of local industry dependent on the industry paying decent wages, Labor was won over to protectionism. Deakin's government, with Labor support, passed a protective tariff in 1908. The tariff barrier was raised further in 1921 and in 1930.

Primary producers were hurt by the tariff; they sold on a world market but had to pay higher prices for goods bought from protected local industries. When the Country Party (the predecessor to the National Party) emerged during the First World War, it wanted to cut back protection. It soon realised this was a lost cause and so settled for 'protection all round', which meant that primary producers were supplied with marketing schemes and subsidies.

These settled policies of the Commonwealth were abandoned in the 1980s and 1990s. Governments cut tariffs, abolished support for primary industries and replaced centralised wage-fixing with bargaining at the enterprise level. Free trade and an open economy became the new settled policy, supported by most economic experts. In the two decades that followed, the economy grew faster than it had before. The economic experts have drawn up a history of Australia's economic performance to support their point of view:

Before 1890: an open economy with high growth	From 1890 to 1980: closed and protected economy with sluggish growth	From 1980 onwards: an open economy with high growth

This view of our economic past has been queried by Ian McLean, the author of *Why Australia Prospered*, a book I have relied on heavily for this chapter. In the first place, the growth was slow rather than sluggish—Australia did not fall very far down the league table, unlike Argentina. How a nation fares will depend on the world economy, especially a nation like Australia that relies heavily on export. When Australia was flourishing in the nineteenth century and more recently, world markets were open. Between the wars they were not, which makes slower growth unsurprising. In these circumstances, building up manufacturing behind a tariff wall was not so misguided. Manufacturing was a large employer, which allowed the population to grow, and despite what is now said about inefficient industries being sheltered by protection, Australian factories were substantial exporters of goods in the 1950s and 1960s. Holdens were being sent to South Africa, New Zealand and South-east Asia. While in recent decades Australia has done well in the export of minerals, it might be no bad thing to keep manufacturing industries alive as a cushion for when the boom runs out.

Likewise with the central control of wages: McLean finds no definite case that it was a substantial drag on productivity, especially when the small size of the domestic market is allowed for. In short, he is not persuaded that the formula of the current experts will always produce good results—or that the contrary policy was so bad.

QUESTION 4
WHY DID THE AUSTRALIAN COLONIES FEDERATE?

THERE WERE THREE ATTEMPTS TO FEDERATE the colonies in the late nineteenth century. The first, promoted by Victoria in 1883, resulted only in the creation of a weak Federal Council, which not all the colonies joined. The second attempt was a one-man effort begun in 1889 by Henry Parkes, the premier of New South Wales; it produced the 1891 Federal Convention. This body created a constitution for a federal government that was not adopted.

The third attempt began in 1893 at a conference of federalists at Corowa, on the Murray River, who hatched a scheme for the people of the colonies to take charge of the process. They would elect delegates to a new constitutional convention, which would write a constitution to be submitted to the people for their approval. With many hiccups, this scheme was

successful. (The key developments are recorded in the chrono-
logical table below.) The Commonwealth was proclaimed on
1 January 1901 before a huge crowd in Sydney's Centennial
Park. The Duke of York, heir to the throne, opened the first
federal parliament in Melbourne on 9 May 1901.

FEDERATION: A BRIEF CHRONOLOGY

1883

Inter-colonial convention meets in Sydney because
of fears of German and French designs in the Pacific.
Agrees to form a federal council.

1885–86

Formation of Federal Council, which has miniscule legislative
powers and no executive power. NSW and SA decline to join.

1889

Henry Parkes, premier of NSW, calls for a
convention to frame a constitution.

1890

Inter-colonial conference agrees to federation in principle
and recommends the calling of a convention.

1891

Federal convention elected by the colonial parliaments
meets and drafts a constitution.

1891–93

Colonial parliaments debate constitution desultorily;
Parkes cannot get support in NSW parliament; proposal lapses.
Collapse of banking and financial institutions;
general depression.

1893

Formation of Federal Leagues in NSW and Vic. Conference
of leagues and the Australian Natives' Association at
Corowa proposes election of new convention by popular vote
and submission of agreed constitution to referendum.

1894

George Reid, premier of NSW, supports
election of new convention.

1895

Conference of premiers agrees to Corowa procedure.

1897

Elections held for ten delegates to convention in NSW, Vic, SA
and Tas; WA parliament appoints its delegates; Qld remains aloof.

1897–98

Convention meets in Adelaide, Sydney and
Melbourne, and adopts constitution.

1898

Voters in Vic, SA and Tas agree to constitution at
referendums; in NSW 'yes' wins narrowly
but fails to reach stipulated minimum of 80,000.

1899

Conference of premiers makes alteration in constitution
to humour NSW (the capital to be in that colony).
Amended constitution agreed to by referendums
in NSW, Vic, Qld, SA and Tas.

1900

Edmund Barton, Alfred Deakin, Charles Kingston,
James Dickson and Philip Fysh, representing the federating
colonies, watch over the passage of the constitution
through the Colonial Office and the British parliament.
Queen Victoria assents to the *Commonwealth of Australia Bill.*
WA agrees to constitution at referendum.

1901

Commonwealth proclaimed in Sydney at Centennial Park,
and Barton and other ministers sworn in.
First federal parliament meets in Melbourne.

When I began to study federation, its relationship with nationalism was set out in this way: a national government promoted national feeling but was not caused by it. I have come to hold the opposite view: without national feeling there would have been no federation.

The no-nationalism view held that federation was chiefly a business deal: it created free trade between the colonies and a common market for Australia, and economic interests were its chief promoters. The politicians who actually did the work invoked the nation in their speeches but this was window-dressing. The constitutional conventions were horse-trading bazaars at which the premiers and their cohorts worked to protect the interests of their colonies. You only have to look at photos of the convention delegates to know that there was no nobility in this work: these are middle-class men in suits with beards, a pitiful sub-group of dead white males.

This view seemed more persuasive because federation had not registered in the national consciousness. If we did not remember it, it can't have been very important to national life. The nation's origins are well known to lie at Gallipoli and its heroes are not Henry Parkes and Edmund Barton but Ned Kelly, Don Bradman and Phar Lap. When the hundredth anniversary of federation was celebrated in 2001, the Australian people had to be told in TV ads that Barton was their first prime minister.

For the anniversary I wrote a book, *The Sentimental Nation*, which was designed to counter this view of federation. What follows are the arguments I assembled.

If federation was a business deal, why was big business in Melbourne opposed to it?

This was one of my early discoveries, and I reckon conclusive. Melbourne was the largest city and the financial centre of the six colonies. There was Melbourne money in Riverina sheep stations and Broken Hill mines, in cattle and sugar in Queensland, in mining on the west coast of Tasmania. Business here, if anywhere, should have been in favour of federation.

My discovery happened in this way. I had decided to begin my study of federation by reading through the *Daily Telegraph*, a Sydney newspaper that was opposed to it. That, I thought, should give me a fresh perspective on an old topic. I was in the State Library of Victoria, reading original copies of the paper in big bound volumes.

In one issue there was a short item on an inter-colonial meeting of the chambers of commerce which seemed to be discussing federation. But there was something odd about the report. I decided I should check the records of the Melbourne chamber. The catalogue told me that the State Library held them, two levels above where I sat. Aren't research libraries wonderful places! In half an hour I was looking at these records. I soon discovered that the leading businessmen who composed the chamber were in favour of a customs union between the colonies but that they were opposed to federation.

The businessmen considered federation much too difficult: a whole constitution would have to be written; the representation in a federal parliament of the different colonies, large and small, would have to be settled; the powers to be yielded to the central government would have to be decided. It would take forever. Politicians who talked of federation were wasting their time. Let's do a customs union first, the businessmen argued, which will bring immediate economic benefits, and do the nation later. Their model was the path to unity that

Germany had taken. A customs union there was established in 1834, and the nation thirty-seven years later, in 1871. This is the path that Europe has taken in our time: a common market first and a political union still to be realised.

The Melbourne businessmen boasted that they were practical men, concerned just with the bottom line. But all their efforts to foster a customs union failed. The chambers of commerce of the capital cities met at a number of inter-colonial conferences. They could agree that customs barriers between the colonies should be abolished, but what policy should be adopted towards the rest of the world? On this question the two leading colonies had adopted different policies: New South Wales had kept to free trade, the British policy, while Victoria had adopted protection to encourage local manufacturing and farming. The merchants of the Melbourne chamber of commerce had opposed protection, but knew that Victoria would not move to federation unless protection was the policy of the new nation. Merchants in free-trade Sydney knew this well enough, which made them highly suspicious of federation. They were always very wary of conferences on a customs union called by the Melbourne chamber. The confer-ences met but differences had to be papered over and no joint action ever followed.

But failure did not deter the Melbourne chamber; it kept up the fantasy that business could agree on the terms of the customs union and then present them to the politicians for implementation. Until very late it opposed federation. The secretary of the Melbourne chamber attended the Corowa conference in 1893; he left disappointed because these enthusiasts had resolved to have another try at federation. It was only when federation looked a strong likelihood that Melbourne business came on board; big business in Sydney remained opposed.

The politicians turned out to be the more practical men. Henry Parkes solved the problem of the two leading colonies disagreeing over trade policy. In his call for federation in 1889 he said that these differences should be laid aside. The national parliament should be formed first, and it should be left to settle trade policy. Differences over the tariff were a 'mere trifle' compared to the duty of founding a nation.

This was a huge risk for the leader of the free-trade party in New South Wales to take. It was one reason why Parkes' plan for federation came unstuck. But the next and successful move to federation operated on the Parkes plan. So the appeal to national feeling trumped differences over economic policy. The nation was made first, and then it delivered the customs union. If there had been no national feeling to appeal to, the stalemate between Victoria and New South Wales would have continued. Parkes died in 1895 but his title of 'father of federation' is well deserved. The first Commonwealth parliament produced a 'compromise' tariff.

**If federation was a business deal,
why did those working for it call it
a 'noble', 'sacred' and 'holy' cause?**

These terms appear not only in public speeches but also in the private papers of the leading federalists. They reflected the belief that nation-building was the way to a better future for the world. It was God's will, or a stage in the evolution of mankind, that all the peoples of the world should have their own state and govern themselves.

Since the wars of the twentieth century, nationalism has looked a dangerous beast; in the nineteenth century it was seen as the way to liberate peoples from tyranny. The great empires of the European landmass—the Russian, Austrian and Turkish—ruled over subject peoples. The Poles, Hungarians, Italians and Romanians, struggling to throw off their imperial overlords, enjoyed the sympathy of liberal, progressive people around the world. Giuseppe Garibaldi, the swashbuckling general of Italian nationalism, had a huge following. In Sydney on his death in 1882, a crowd of 10,000 gathered in the Exhibition Building to mourn him. The Italian float in the federal procession in Sydney on 1 January 1901 carried a bust of Henry Parkes surrounded by Italian soldiers, two of whom were dressed like Garibaldi's redshirts. The liberal hope was that when all nations were governing themselves, they would come together in a world federation, which would bring peace at last. Lord Tennyson, the British poet laureate, sang of 'the parliament of man, the Federation of the world'.

The federalists in Australia saw their cause as part of this world movement. They were not planning to throw off an oppressor; this was to be a self-governing nation under the British crown. But federation in Australia meant the breaking down of local jealousies and divisions, and the leading of the people into the higher life of nationhood. Instead of being a collection of colonies, Australia would take its place among the other nations of the globe and the march of progress to better things.

This was a cause to which federalists were devoted with a religious fervour. The first two prime ministers of the Commonwealth, Edmund Barton and Alfred Deakin, believed they were doing God's will in working for federation.

If federation was a business deal, why was there so much poetry?

The scholar who prepared a bibliography of writings on federation decided to spare us the poetry. At one level this was understandable: there was a lot of it, mostly poor and very repetitive. But in excluding it, he took the heart out of the federation movement. The poetry embodied the vision for the new nation: why it should be formed and what sort of nation it would be. That the poetry was repetitious shows how well established the vision was; that people who should never have written poetry composed it shows how moving was this cause. This poetry was not hidden away in literary journals; it appeared in the newspapers, was quoted in federalist speeches, was set to music in support of the 'yes' cause at the referendums and was officially encouraged by a prize in 1901.

What became the Australian national anthem, 'Advance Australia Fair', composed in 1878, comes from this school of poetry. Its most puzzling line, 'our land is girt by sea', was a standard image and in 1878 needed no explanation. The poets considered that Australia, sharing no land borders with other powers and set apart in its own realm, was made for nationhood. Protected by the girdle of the sea, its virtues could flourish unmolested. The words *girt*, *girdling*, *girdle* and *girdled* were applied as sense and rhythm demanded. Here is a verse from one of the bad federation poems composed by Henry Parkes:

> *God girdled our majestic isle*
> *With seas far-reaching east and west,*
> *That man might live beneath this smile*
> *In peace and freedom ever blest.*

'Freedom' was an Australian characteristic, said Parkes. 'Young and free', says the national anthem. These, too, were standard themes. The freedom Australians enjoyed was, in the first place, the traditional British freedoms, but in Australia extended to more people: all men could vote. Australia was also superior to Britain because it lacked the barriers of a rigid class system. Opportunity was open to all and there was no inherited privilege. Again, 'Advance Australia Fair' gives this theme in

shorthand form, 'wealth for toil', which carried a double mean-
ing: there was the opportunity to make money and, implicitly,
wealth comes only from toil.

The 'peace' in Parkes' verse was not simply freedom from
external aggression. The poets celebrated Australian society
as unified and hence peaceful: the people were of one stock or
blood or race; they spoke one language; there were no ongoing
feuds; and, most surprising to us, no blood had been spilt. The
frontier battles with the Aborigines were well enough known
(the silence or evasion on this matter came later), but Aborigines were assumed to be dying out and so did not register in the
national vision. Warfare constantly renewed was the experience Australia was spared.

Australia is young and female in these poems, fresh and virginal. She receives extensive treatment in this guise in one of the
better poems, by John Farrell, a Sydney journalist and editor:

> We have no records of a by-gone shame,
> No red-writ histories of woe to weep:
> God set our land in summer seas asleep
> Till His fair morning for her waking came.
>
> He hid her where the rage of Old World wars
> Might never break upon her virgin rest:
> He sent His softest winds to fan her breast,
> And canopied her night with low-hung stars.

He wrought her perfect, in a happy clime,
And held her worthiest, and bade her wait
Serene on her lone couch inviolate
The heightened manhood of a later time.

The men worthy to take Australia, the 'manful pioneers', only
leave Europe when freedom has dawned there:

They found a gracious amplitude of soil,
Unsown with memories, like poison weeds,
Of far-forefathers' wrongs and vengeful deeds,
Where was no crown, save that of earnest toil.

They reared a sunnier England, where the pain
Of bitter yesterdays might not arise:
They said—'The past is past, and all its cries,
Of time-long hatred are beyond the main ...

'And, with fair peace's white, pure flag unfurled,
Our children shall, upon this new-won shore—
Warned by all sorrows that have gone before—
Build up the glory of a grand New World.'

A 'grand New World': there is not much of this in the prosaic
language of the Australian constitution—except in the name of
the new nation, the Commonwealth. This represented an Australian ideal of the state: it existed not to enrich or aggrandise

an elite or to embark on conquest, but to serve the common-weal, the common good. The prize-winning poem in the 1901 competition, written by George Essex Evans, linked the name to the standard themes:

> *Free-born of Nations, Virgin white,*
> *Not won by blood nor ringed with steel,*
> *Thy throne is on a loftier height*
> *Deep-rooted in the Commonweal!*

This nationalist poetry is now lost to us—except for the national anthem, which is far from being the best example. The usual account of our literature is that the nationalist school began in the 1890s with the works of A. B. 'Banjo' Paterson and Henry Lawson. Their works sold well in the 1890s but no one thought their poems were fit for the celebration of the nation. Nor could anyone then imagine that the nation would come to value most a song about a sheep-stealing swagman and a poem on the exploits of a Snowy Mountains horseman. These writers gave Australians masculine figures to admire who had nothing to do with the public life of the country. The poets who had written of the ideals that should sustain national life rendered Australia as female, a pure young woman.

If, in judging the role of nationalism in federation, we try to imagine the founding fathers singing 'Waltzing Matilda', we will get the wrong answer. The founders did know of the pure young woman and all she stood for.

If federation was a business deal,
why was it run as a democratic crusade?

The constitution written in 1891 was the work of a convention whose members had been elected by the colonial parliaments. It went back to the parliaments for their consideration. In New South Wales, Parkes could not give it priority because part of his free-trade party was unhappy with it, while the new Labor Party, which held the balance of power, was not interested at all. There was some discussion in the other parliaments, but without New South Wales there was little point in proceeding.

The plan to have the people elect the delegates to a new convention, and for the people rather than the parliaments to pass judgement on the constitution, was designed to lift the cause out of normal politics. There would be a defined process with which the politicians could not interfere. But this open, democratic method was also appealing because in the 1890s there was already a movement to make the colonial constitutions more thoroughly democratic. The federal movement became its standard-bearer, and it did produce an ultra-democratic constitution for the new nation. The anti-democrats who wanted federation had to swallow down their conservative principles, lie back and think of Australia.

The democracy of the 1850s could scarcely speak its name. It was suspect as anti-British and subversive. As we have seen in Question 2, the chief cause behind the widening of the franchise was the inflation of property values, which gave more people the vote without the law being changed. Manhood suffrage was granted but hedged around: you had to be an established resident of the electorate, and the old qualifications for the vote survived so that if you owned property in a number of electorates you had a vote for them all. This was known as plural voting. There was no payment of members. Powerful upper houses in Victoria, Tasmania and South Australia were elected on a narrow property franchise. In New South Wales and Queensland, upper houses were nominated which gave liberal governments some chance of having the governor nominate new members if their measures were being obstructed. Women did not possess the vote and in the 1850s no one proposed that they should.

By 1890 all the colonies had begun paying their members of parliament. This had been pushed chiefly by country people so that they did not have to rely on electing men who lived in the capital city. Its immediate effect was to allow the trade unions to form an effective labour party. Their members could not have entered parliament without payment. Asking unionists to contribute funds to pay for a member was never going to be reliable.

In the twenty years after 1890, progressive liberals with Labor support did chalk up a number of democratic victories. Plural voting was abolished. Residential qualifications for the vote were reduced. Women gained the right to vote. The referendum, the method of direct democracy, was used in South Australia to test opinion on Bible reading in schools and reform of the upper house. Reforming of upper houses did not get very far. They were prepared to widen their electorates, though still requiring a property test for the vote, but not to reduce their powers.

Of these victories, the vote for women was the most spectacular. South Australia adopted this first, in 1894, which made it a world leader, one year behind New Zealand and not far behind the western states of the United States, which were the first to make this change. The feminist history books list the undoubted disadvantages and discrimination women suffered in Australia, but these will not explain why women gained the vote so early in Australia. If oppression alone explained success, feminism would have flourished first in the Middle East.

The key is that most women in Australia had achieved an enhanced position in the home: they were in charge of domestic affairs and the children. The patriarchy outside the home then rankled more; when their half-liberated wives and daughters demanded the vote, it was hard for the menfolk to refuse them. The women's movement in Australia played on women's role as homemakers and mothers to get the vote; it did not demand access to all male jobs or to parliament itself. That prospect was what frightened the men, and why, in the United Kingdom and in the eastern United States, the reform was opposed much longer.

The progressive liberals who were in a majority at the constitutional convention of 1897–98 would have liked to have given women the vote for the Commonwealth. But since only South Australia had so far adopted the change, they feared this was pushing the matter too hard. They snuck the women in by a cunning ploy. At the first Commonwealth election the franchise was to be the existing colonial franchises. Thereafter, the Commonwealth could make its own electoral law, but in doing so it could not deprive anyone of the vote who already had it. South Australian women already had the vote; if the Commonwealth was to have a uniform law, then the South Australian practice would have to become the Australian practice. Which is what happened under the first Commonwealth electoral law in 1902.

On other matters, the constitutional convention wrote the new democratic measures into the constitution. There was to be no plural voting. Payment of members was to operate for both houses of parliament (in some colonies members of upper houses were not paid). The voters for the Senate, the upper house, were to be the same as for the lower house. (After 1902 this meant a universal franchise for both houses.) To ultra-democrats, a Senate which had equal representation of the states was undemocratic, which was the chief reason why the Labor Party opposed federation, but an upper house elected on a democratic franchise was unheard of. At this time the United States' Senate was still elected by the state congresses. Since liberals had been thwarted by upper houses in colonial politics, the constitution provided a system for resolving deadlocks between the houses: an election for both houses, and then, if necessary, a joint sitting to resolve the matter in dispute. (There has been only one joint sitting, in 1974, which was how Gough Whitlam's Labor government established Medibank, the precursor to Medicare, against determined Liberal opposition.) Finally, any changes to the constitution were to be decided by the people at a referendum; this was regarded as an ultra-democratic measure, though it has turned out to be a conservative one. The makers of the constitution assumed an informed electorate and did not foresee the force of the slogan 'If in doubt, vote no'.

The constitutional convention of 1897–98 was meant to start afresh on writing a constitution. In practice, it worked from the 1891 document drafted by Samuel Griffith, the then premier of Queensland. The chief changes made were those that made the federal parliament more democratic. They are set out in the table on page 108. They indicate the growing strength of the democratic movement and the impossibility of achieving federation on anything other than a democratic basis. Conservative upper houses in the colonies might thwart reform but the new nation was to be democratic from the jump.

Before the Commonwealth could come into existence, the people had to agree via a referendum to accept a document with 128 clauses. There was a 'no' campaign with the exaggerations, scares and lies to which we are accustomed. Nevertheless, the 'yes' cause prevailed.

The federalists took great pride in their achievement. This federation was not created by military might or the need to unite against an external threat. The Australian people had freely voted to make themselves into a united commonwealth because they saw the benefits that union would bring. What prospects lay before a nation with this pedigree!

DEMOCRATISING THE CONSTITUTION
Comparing the 1891 and 1897–98 drafts

The drafts established two Houses with American names:
a House of Representatives, elected by the people, and a Senate,
with the same number of senators from each state.

	1891	1897–98
House of Representatives	Elected on state franchise.	After first election, Commonwealth sets own franchise; no one with vote in states can be excluded. (Result: all men and women get the vote.) No plural voting.
Senate	Elected by state parliaments.	Elected by same people as House of Representatives.
Resolving deadlocks	(No provision.)	If Senate twice rejects a bill, both Houses dissolved and election for whole parliament; if bill still blocked, joint sitting of houses and majority wins.
Amending constitution	By state conventions.	By referendum.

Are economic interests to be left out of this account? Certainly not. Once federation was in prospect, individuals and businesses considered how it would benefit or harm them. The treasurers of the colonial governments were very alert to how federation would affect their budgets, since the central government was now to collect customs duties, which had been one of the colonies' mainstays. All these interests were active as the constitution was being drawn up and in the campaigns for its adoption. At the referendums there is a clear pattern of the 'no' vote rising in places which looked as if they would be harmed by free trade between the states, and of the 'yes' vote rising where there was a clear advantage. But these interests did not create the demand for federation. It was the federalist politicians, poets and patriots who were devoted to the cause and worked to achieve it. What was their interest?

They certainly had an interest, though not an economic one. They were interested in the enhanced status that would come to them by belonging to a nation. Whenever Griffith was asked why he supported federation, he answered that he was sick of being a colonial. To be colonial was to be a second-rate, marginal figure; you were defined by your subordinate relationship with a mother country. Griffith, supremely able and highly ambitious, did not want to be taken as inferior. In the constitution he drafted, the word 'colony' disappeared. The colonies became states in a new Commonwealth of Australia, to which Griffith gave all the powers of a nation. Defence and external affairs were listed as Commonwealth powers, even though the oversight of these matters rested for the moment with Britain.

In one of his great speeches, in 1889 Henry Parkes expressed the hurt he and others felt from their colonial status:

> Instead of a confusion of names and geographical divisions, which so perplexes many people at a distance, we shall be Australians, and a people with 7,000 miles of coast, more than 2,000,000 square miles of land, with 4,000,000 of population, and shall present ourselves to the world as 'Australia' ... We shall have a higher stature before the world. We shall have a grander name.

For Parkes himself, the other advantage of federation was that he could cap his long career as a colonial premier by being the first prime minister of the Australian nation.

There was one group of people who felt their colonial status most keenly: the first generation born in Australia, the 'natives' so called. Their parents were colonials but at least they'd been born in the mother country. The natives were inferior both by birth and by residence. In Victoria from the 1870s, native-born young men ran the Australian Natives' Association to fight against the slurs they suffered. Their parents and all the people of consequence in Victorian society were gold-rush immigrants of the 1850s. As is common, this generation found many faults in the upcoming generation, which in this case had a simple explanation: they were native-born. The young

Australians were criticised for being sports-mad, mentally lazy, disrespectful of authority and great swearers. The natives set out to show that they were sober citizens, fine achievers in many realms, and to contest the notion that if a professor or an archbishop was to be appointed he had to come from the old country. They defended colonial products against the usual prejudice against them, whether they were wine or poetry.

The Natives' Association ran a medical insurance scheme similar to those run by the lodges, which gave them a sure base of support. At their local meetings, after the insurance business was disposed of, they ran debates, lectures and mock courts—anything that would help with self-improvement and give the lie to their detractors. They did allow alcohol, but not gambling.

In the 1880s they committed themselves to the cause of federation. If a nation could be formed, their deepest purpose would be realised—for who had a greater claim to respect in a nation than the people born in it? They were a Victorian organisation which now had a national outlook. They saw the contradiction and set about to create branches in the other colonies. By 1890 there were branches in all the mainland colonies, though none was as strong as the Victorian, where the clash between the generations was most clear-cut. The Natives' Association was the one Australian body committed to federation in good times and bad, and ever ready to do the legwork to bring the cause to fruition. Barton kept a list of its branches beside him for reference.

Historians note that the turnout at the federation referendums was lower than at ordinary elections—voting was voluntary—and conclude that there was a lot of apathy on the question. No one knew this better than those who worked to get out the 'yes' vote. The historians are in error when they conclude from this that nationalism cannot have been a strong force in federation. National feeling does not have to be universal to be influential. It takes hold first on some groups rather than others. The native-born had a special need for an Australian nation.

*

When I was a university student, historians commonly looked to economic forces to explain events. It is that view of federation that I have been contesting. Now historians are very interested in race and national identity. This has led to the claim that the chief purpose of federation was to establish the White Australia policy.

At first glance, this claim has a lot going for it. The first substantial measure the new federal parliament passed was the *Immigration Restriction Act*, which was the legislative basis for the White Australia policy. In supporting the measure, Alfred Deakin, the attorney-general and deputy prime minister, asserted that the chief motive for federation was the desire of the Australian people, acting together through a national government, to protect their racial purity. These were his words:

No motive power operated more universally on this continent or in the beautiful island of Tasmania, and certainly
no motive power operated more powerfully in dissolving
the technical and arbitrary political divisions which previously separated us than did the desire that we should be one
people and remain one people without the admixture of
other races.

Deakin was well placed to speak about the federation campaign because he had devoted himself to it throughout the
1890s. He led the campaign in Victoria. The only other man
who had done more for the cause was Edmund Barton, who
led the campaign in New South Wales. Deakin is an attrac-
tive character. He was a profound scholar of the religions of
the world; he sought nothing for himself out of public life; he
was free of the cruder forms of race prejudice; he was the best
of the enlightened progressive liberals who made the Commonwealth. He was also a clever politician, and these eloquent
words turn out to be totally misleading.

This is the conclusion reached by Ron Norris, who sub-
jected this claim of Deakin to very close scrutiny in his book
The Emergent Commonwealth. Norris looked first at the conferences and conventions which were responsible for the writing
of the constitution. At none of these meetings was immigration an important issue. Amid all the arguments advanced for
why the colonies should federate, control of immigration simply did not rate. The new Commonwealth was to have power

over immigration, but even here there was no sense that this was a matter crying out for national attention. In the 1891 constitution the Commonwealth was to have exclusive power over immigration; in 1897–98 the states and the Commonwealth were both to have power. The founders were envisaging that immigration could go on being a matter controlled by the states; only later would Commonwealth action be necessary.

In the referendum campaigns, extravagant claims and extravagant fears were peddled. Again, the need for national action on immigration did not rate. During the campaign, a Chinese hawker in South Australia was discovered to have leprosy. There was an outcry about this, but no one used the case to show that a national government was needed to take strong action against the Chinese.

The reason for this almost total lack of interest is obvious. The colonies had each passed more or less uniform laws against the Chinese in 1888, which went close to prohibiting Chinese immigration. Some colonies had widened the net in the 1890s and moved against the Indians and Japanese as well, using the device of a dictation test, which was the method used by the Commonwealth in 1901. The problem of Asian immigration had already been solved.

Had it not been solved, it is difficult to imagine that the Chinese would have been allowed to take such a prominent part in the federal celebrations in Melbourne in May 1901. The Chinese merchants of Little Bourke Street put up an arch and used it to get the street decorations extended to their quarter.

Two days before the opening of the new federal parliament, 200,000 people watched a Chinese procession pass through the city streets.

So why the swift action against Chinese and other Asian immigration as soon as the parliament assembled?

The ministers who were sworn in on 1 January 1901 had to declare a policy on the vexed issue of the tariff. This was a pressing matter. The inter-colonial trade barriers could come down only when the Commonwealth established what uniform duties were to be collected at the ports. Barton's government was protectionist, but for the first election it declared for only moderate protection. The opposition leader, George Reid, was campaigning for free trade.

The tariff was divisive and tricky. The new government wanted to go to the people with a popular rallying cry, and in particular with something on which it could compete successfully with the Labor Party, the new third party, which was neutral on the tariff. Workingmen and their unions had always been in the forefront of the demand for a White Australia, and the Labor Party had a White Australia at the top of its platform.

This explains why the Barton government went to the people at the first federal election promising to legislate for a White Australia. The results of the election pushed it to honour that promise. Protectionists and free-traders were close to equal in their parliamentary strength. The balance of power would be held by the Labor Party. Some of their members were protectionists, some free-traders—but all would support a government which was legislating for a White Australia.

The government had to pretend it was responding to some real need on the immigration front. It called for figures on the level of Asian immigration. Ten persons had invaded South Australia since 1899; 133 had swarmed into the Northern Territory, but 151 had left; and 304 Japanese had descended into Queensland since 1898, but 864 had left. Though clearly there was no pressing need, the defining of the nation by the composition of its people made a fitting opening to the Commonwealth's career.

Much more decisive in ensuring a White Australia was the government's decision to phase out the use of Pacific Islanders as indentured labourers on the Queensland cane fields. This was announced by Barton in his policy speech and became the chief issue in the federal election in Queensland. The system had been a matter of contention in Queensland for years. It had been marked down for extinction and then reprieved. Labor in Queensland was fiercely opposed to it but had no influence, since a grand coalition of all Labor's opponents ruled the colony.

The sugar planters had supported federation, since it would open an Australia-wide market for their sugar, but had hoped that any move against their labour force would be delayed. Barton's immediate move against it outraged them and the Queensland government. The last labourers were to be returned to their islands by 1906. The Commonwealth placed a duty on imported sugar to protect the industry, and an excise was placed on local production, which would be lifted if the planter used white labour. It was a great victory for White Australia when it turned out that white labour on award wages could grow sugar in the tropics.

The origins of the term 'White Australia' are obscure. It was certainly coined in the context of an immigration policy directed against Asians. But from our previous discussion of the national poetry, it should be clear why White Australia was such an effective slogan: it caught the pure and virginal themes already present in the national ideal.

The Chinese were seen as a threat to this. Their blood was not British blood. They were inevitably going to be treated as inferiors and, hence, introduce a caste barrier into Australian society and rob it of social harmony. The Chinese would take work at low wages and threaten the high standard of living of the working class. The anti-Chinese agitation popularised the national ideal and gave it, of course, a much stronger racial element. White was not merely a symbol; it was the colour of the citizens' skins.

Let us return to Deakin. If we think of federation instrumentally, as an arrangement designed to achieve certain objects, then we will say that the desire to exclude the Chinese had little to do with it. But if we think of federation as the realisation of a national ideal, then the exclusion of the Chinese is very definitely part of the story. The agitation against the Chinese gave new power and cogency to the ideal of a pure, pristine, unsullied, united Australia. And that ideal led the federalists onwards. They did want to 'be one people and remain one people without the admixture of other races'.

*

The debased view of the origins of federation began with the Labor Party and its supporters. Formed in the early 1890s, the Labor Party took no part in the making of the constitution. There was one working-class representative at the federal convention of 1897–98. In New South Wales and Victoria, Labor opposed the constitution chiefly because of the equal representation given to the states in the Senate. The 'backward' states of Western Australia and Tasmania, where there was as yet no Labor Party, were to elect the same number of senators as the two big states. The Commonwealth looked like an anti-democratic machine that would stifle Labor's progress.

But in the new Commonwealth parliament the Labor Party was amazingly successful, winning seats in both houses in all states, including Tasmania and Western Australia. After the 1910 election it had a majority in both houses, and its highest vote occurred in Tasmania. In 1909 the free-traders and protectionists were forced to amalgamate into the Liberal Party in an effort to stop the Labor advance.

By the time Labor took office in 1910 under Andrew Fisher, it knew that the interpretations given to the constitution by the High Court would not allow it to implement two key parts of its platform: the control of wages and working conditions throughout the country, and the nationalisation of monopolies. In 1911 it put to the people at a constitutional referendum sweeping proposals to increase Commonwealth power and was defeated. It put the same proposals in 1913 and came much closer to success. (For a constitutional amendment to pass, it requires a majority national vote and a positive vote in a majority of states.) When Labor was again strong during the Second World War, it submitted to the people another raft of proposals to increase Commonwealth power and lost again. Labor's 1947 legislation to nationalise the banks was ruled unconstitutional by the High Court. The constitution quite unambiguously gave the Commonwealth power over banking, but the court ruled that a Commonwealth takeover of the banks was counter to the stipulation of Section 92 that trade and commerce between the states 'shall be absolutely free'.

Labor's battle with the constitution led it to write into its platform its opposition to a federal constitution for Australia. It wanted the Senate abolished and a proper national government to be granted full powers. It only dropped these positions in the 1970s. Since then, the High Court has reinterpreted the constitution and given greatly increased powers to the Commonwealth. A federal government can now nationalise monopolies and the banks, but Labor has lost altogether its appetite for such measures.

It is not surprising that the Labor Party could not think well of the constitution-making of the 1890s. Its supporters and sympathisers in the academy, drawing on the Marxist view that the economic interests of classes are the driving force of history, cast the founding fathers of the federation as middle-class men protecting their interests. They were alleged to have created a Commonwealth government of limited powers so that socialism would be impossible to realise. In an influential textbook, Finlay Crisp, who had worked for Ben Chifley's Labor government, characterised the fathers as 'men of property' and read their motivations from that fact. He it was who, in assembling a bibliography of federation writings, decided to omit all the poetry.

Since federation was the only acceptable route to union, an all-powerful central government could not have been created in 1901. Labor's opposition to the constitution in the 1890s did not concern limited central powers but rather, as we have seen, equal representation of the states in the Senate.

The Labor Party, though sometimes it thinks so, is not the whole nation. Surely others would come to the defence of the constitution-makers? What happened to the honouring of the nation created by an open, peaceful, democratic process? All memory of that passed away.

The forgetting began at the time the federal movement reached its goal. In 1899 the British Empire went to war in South Africa against the Boer republics. The Australian colonies sent soldiers who acquitted themselves well; British commanders were keen to have in their units the mounted horsemen from the Australian bush. There was much more interest in the Boer War and the feats and sacrifices of Australian soldiers than there was in the last stages of the federal movement.

The makers of the federation made a virtue of the absence of military glory in the creation of Australia, but they could not stamp out its allure. The Commonwealth was, after all, baptised by blood. Why the nation could come to think of its birth as occurring at Gallipoli in 1915 rather than in a Sydney park in 1901 was already evident. Though its title might not suggest it, the next chapter will treat the landing at Gallipoli.

WHAT EFFECT DID CONVICT ORIGINS HAVE ON NATIONAL CHARACTER?

W HAT TO ME SEEMS THE MOST CHALLENGING question in Australian history receives commonly a very confident answer. What effect did the convicts have on our national character? Answer: they made us an anti-authoritarian people.

The best antidote to this view is still an article written forty years ago by Henry Reynolds, before he turned his attention to Aboriginal history. He deals with the aftermath of convict transportation in Tasmania and, unusually in historical enquiry, argues with the simplicity and conclusiveness of a syllogism. In Tasmania the convicts represented a higher proportion of the population than on the mainland. If convicts are responsible for an anti-authoritarian attitude, it should be particularly prevalent there. In fact, Tasmania after transportation was the most conservative, traditional and Anglophile of the colonies, the most un-Australian in outlook, with a working class that was submissive, unprotesting and apolitical. Therefore, convicts cannot be responsible for anti-authoritarianism.

Reynolds had in his sights the classic work on the national character by Russel Ward, *The Australian Legend*, published in 1958. Long before Australian society generally accepted and even boasted of its convict foundations, Ward took pleasure in insisting that convicts are our 'founding fathers', and from them he derived our independence, anti-authoritarianism and the group solidarity of men, which became mateship. But he also outlined other factors which accentuated and embedded these characteristics. In the colonies generally, and in particular 'up the country', where the old hands (convicts and ex-convicts) were concentrated, there was a shortage of labour, which removed from workers the fear of the boss. In the pastoral country outback, men wandered independently from station to station, not bound to one employer, often known only by a nickname, and not needing references to land a job. The sparseness of settlement and the isolation from civilised society led these men to depend on one another. Their bonds were more intense because there were few white women in the bush; the pattern of these men's lives was to work hard, drink away their earnings, swear outrageously and find sexual release with Aboriginal women.

It is said that a good history book will carry the evidence to refute its own argument. Perhaps all these other factors that Ward presents were enough to produce the national characteristics? And so convicts can be dropped from the explanation? The Tasmanian case seems to support such a conclusion: here, there was not a labour shortage, settlement was closer and governments and the employing class exercised a firm control on the lower orders.

However, convict influence might be saved by arguing that Australia inherited convict characteristics, but that they needed certain circumstances in which to flourish—New South Wales had them, Tasmania did not. But doubt can be thrown on this supposition, and with an argument that Ward half-recognises. Australia in its foundation years acquired free British workers as well as convicts, and both came from a Britain where the old social bonds of deference were weakening with the disturbances brought about by rapid economic growth and industrialisation. In the late eighteenth century the working people of the towns were known as the 'loose disorderly sort' and were notorious in Europe for their unruliness. By the early nineteenth century, working people were beginning to organise to claim political rights, to be part of the nation and not merely to be the poor or the lower orders. If we find stroppy workers in Australia, we don't have to look for convict influence.

William Howitt, a traveller to the goldfields in the 1850s, was alert for rude behaviour from the lower orders. In England he was a radical but a gentleman, and in Australia he travelled heavy and dressed as a gentleman. On one occasion a group of diggers put him and his son in danger by playing cricket in the middle of the main road. The bowler hurled the ball just past the ear of Howitt's horse, and the batsman struck it back so that it nearly hit his son in the face. Some mounted police had just ridden by and had made no attempt to stop the game. Howitt quietly remonstrated with the men on the danger they were causing, but they heaped abuse on him and yelled, 'We do as we like here. You are not in England, remember.' These men were almost certainly fresh off the boat, as was Howitt himself. Though he was annoyed, he was calm in his explanation of their behaviour, which made no reference to convicts and their influence. He saw them as Englishmen crudely asserting their freedom after being held in more restraint at home.

It is possible in Britain itself to find a workforce with the 'Australian' characteristics without any convict influence. The navvies who built the railways in the early nineteenth century were high-paid, roving men, often known only by a nickname, who spent their monthly wages in a great burst of drinking and being a great terror to decent society. They were a tribe apart and had strong loyalty to one another: a navvy on the tramp between jobs would camp with other navvies, who were honour-bound to contribute funds to see him on his way. Like the Australian sundowners, some of these trampers were suspected of never wanting to find a job.

Are we done with convicts? Not quite, because we need to consider the quintessential anti-authority figure, the Irish convict. Ward puts much stress on him. Since the Irish were rebels against foreign domination and tyrannical landlords, they seem natural candidates as contributors to Australian anti-authoritarianism. But this mistakes the nature of the anti-authoritarian attitude we are discussing. We are not looking for explanations for open, violent rebellion. There has been little of that in Australia, and when it did occur—at Castle Hill, near Sydney, in convict times, and at Eureka, on the Ballarat goldfields—the Irish were prominent. We are looking for the origins of a street-smart, irreverent attitude, mocking authority or evading authority but with no sense of controlling or replacing it. The origins of this are English, late-eighteenth-century, working-class and urban; not pre-modern, rural and Irish. The Irish were more communal and tribal, more combative and loyal, less interested in independence and swagger, and pleased to find a patron who would protect them: 'God bless you, your honour.'

The Australian national character is always presented as a marked departure from the character of the English. When Australians make these comparisons they are thinking of the toffy, upper-crust Englishman in a bowler hat. When George Orwell described the English national character in 1940, he wrote of the working class and the lower middle class—the very people who came to Australia.

> ... another English characteristic which is so much a part of
> us that we barely notice it ... is the addiction to hobbies and

spare-time occupations, the *privateness* of English life. We are
a nation of flower-lovers, but also a nation of stamp-collectors,
pigeon-fanciers, amateur carpenters, coupon-snippers, darts-
players, crossword-puzzle fans. All the culture that is most
truly native centres round things which even when they are
communal are not official—the pub, the football match, the
back garden, the fireside and the 'nice cup of tea'. The liberty
of the individual is still believed in, almost as in the nineteenth century. But this has nothing to do with economic
liberty, the right to exploit others for profit. It is the liberty
to have a home of your own, to do what you like in your spare
time, to choose your own amusements instead of having
them chosen for you from above ...

One thing one notices if one looks directly at the common people, especially in the big towns, is that they are not
puritanical. They are inveterate gamblers, drink as much
beer as their wages will permit, are devoted to bawdy jokes,
and use probably the foulest language in the world.

Much of this is true of Australians, and of Australians who are
no longer working-class. The drinking, gambling and swearing
are part of the national stereotype that Ward identified and
explored; he did not recognise as part of the national character
the desire for the back garden and the home of your own, but
they have been highlighted by those who have labelled Australia the first suburban nation. Nationalists writing of national
character look for distinctiveness of local origin; we are better

off thinking that Australian characteristics are those of the English working class writ large.

Ward considers that the outback workers—shearers, stockmen, drovers—adopted in the purest form the national characteristics that interest him. Yet it was the city larrikins, whom he does not mention, who made anti-authoritarianism an art form and who set a style which has become nationally admired. Larrikins flourished in the last decades of the nineteenth century and at first were not lovable people. Their pushes operated openly: they blocked the footpaths, jostled passers-by, made obscene remarks to respectable girls and women, and spat on the clothes of well-dressed men. They beat up and robbed drunks and Chinese. But they were different from the roughs of European towns. The Melbourne journalist John Stanley James described them in this way:

> One marked difference between the Melbourne larrikin
> and his compeers elsewhere is his extreme boldness and
> contempt of authorities. In Europe, the 'rough' avoids
> the neighbourhood of police courts. He loves not to be
> known by magistrates or detectives. But here, the larrikin
> not only chaffs and annoys the policeman on his beat, but
> daily crowds the police court, and manifests the liveliest
> interest in the fate of male or female friends who may be
> on trial ... Another marked difference, which is in the lar-
> rikin's favour, is his generally better-fed and better-clothed
> appearance. The rowdy and thief in the old world, after all,

lead a miserable life, and generally their profession does not appear to be a lucrative one; but here, in the first stage, they seem physically in good shape.

When tough measures against larrikins were called for, the larrikins were often found to be the children of respectable parents and in work. When they were prosecuted they could raise the money to employ a lawyer in their defence. The larrikin spirit is still a mysterious phenomenon. It was not the defiance of the damaged and excluded; it was the boldness that came from self-confidence, of young men who would not be confined.

A prosperous working class, free of old-world condescension, had spawned in its native-born youth this baroque display of independence. In Sydney it was possible to argue that the larrikins were a residue from convict times, but larrikins flourished in all cities, and particularly in Melbourne, the largest, which had only a faint convict heritage.

*

The strongest influence of the convicts is not to be sought in the anti-authoritarian attitudes of a segment of the people, but in the trauma of a nation which had to come to terms with its shameful origins. How was Australia to cope with the world's bad opinion? The one thing that everyone knew about Australia was that it was founded with convicts, which continued to make it morally suspect. As an 1850 British verse had it:

There vice is virtue, virtue vice
And all that's vile is voted nice

The world would not forget the convict past, though Australians had themselves disowned it with the anti-transportation movement of the 1840s. When the crowd at the Sydney Cricket Ground invaded the pitch in 1879, an Englishman at the crease called out, 'You sons of convicts!' In 1942 Winston Churchill was tired of John Curtin's requests about the need for British reinforcements for Australia and blamed this panic on 'bad stock'.

For over a century Australians upheld a taboo of not mentioning the convicts. This covered the shame; it did not remove it. My exploration here of the consequences of this repression is necessarily speculative, but there is no doubt about how raw this wound was. In 1899 a well-intentioned governor of New South Wales, en route to take up his post, sent this message ahead: 'Greeting; your birth stain have you turned to good.' There was an uproar and the governor had to retreat from such an offensive remark.

As we have seen in Question 4, in the late nineteenth century the image of Australia in verse and picture was of a young virginal girl, absolutely pure. The purity came from being free of the old-world ills of caste, inequality and class prejudice: Australians were one people on a single continent, living in harmony with no civil strife, with opportunity for all, isolated from the rest of the world by the encircling sea. I think this stress on the nation's purity was the Australian response to the impure origins of the nation. 'You think we are polluted,' the poets are saying to the world, 'but we are developing a nation that is superior to all others.' The purity and the whiteness did not at first refer to race. This image was developed before Asian migration was taken to be a threat. It was not until the late 1880s that the nation-to-be was taking a racial form; the colonies first cooperated to limit Chinese migration in 1888. Thereafter, the slogan of 'White Australia' carried all the hopes for the young nation: pure, progressive, enlightened.

Other nations excluded Asian immigrants but not under a slogan of the Australian type—a 'White New Zealand' or a 'White Canada' did not become the panoply of nationhood. Racial purity was more desperately sought and proclaimed in Australia. Increasingly around the world purity of race mattered, and on that test Australia could rate high: Australians boasted they were ninety-eight per cent British, free of the mixture of other races. The insistence on this, the boastfulness about it, was the way to show the world that the convict stain had been washed away—except, of course, that in racial thought blood went on counting, so in hitching Australia's destiny to a purity of race, the Australians did not escape their origins, as Churchill's jibe about bad blood showed.

Purity of race is no longer a progressive cause, as it was in 1900, but democracy still is. In the disowning of the racism of White Australia, we can overlook that it advanced the cause of a more democratic Australia, in two senses. Firstly, a racial identity obliterates the differences of class within the nation.

All men are 'white men', a common bond of masculinity, which took on a moral dimension as a 'white man' became one who was true-hearted, loyal, reliable. Secondly, racial exclusion had been demanded most vociferously by working people, their trade unions and the early Labor Party. Workers would be the ones to suffer most directly if cheap 'coloured' labour became prevalent. The acceptance of their demand for the exclusion of Asians was a commitment by the nation to the dignity of labour and its proper reward.

Here is another speculative connection between convict shame and national history. The landing at Gallipoli has been honoured more and more fervently in recent years, but the claim, made at the time, that the nation was born at Gallipoli is a puzzle to modern Australians. Did Gallipoli mean so much because it was a supreme test of Australian mateship? No. Did Australians honour it because they took a perverse delight in defeat? No. Gallipoli did make the nation because it freed it from the self-doubt about whether it had the mettle to be a proper nation. Australian soldiers had been put to the supreme test and had come through magnificently. Landed at the wrong place, facing almost perpendicular cliffs with the Turks firing on them from above, they got ashore and scrambled up and hung on. All the military experts proclaimed their success; most importantly, the British praised them. The first description of the landing to be published in Australian newspapers came from the British war correspondent Ellis Ashmead-Bartlett. His praise was worth much more than that of the

Australian war correspondent, C. E. W. Bean, which arrived later. Ashmead-Bartlett's report (see below) is a foundation document of Australian nationality. Once Australians read it, they knew they had gained a good name before the world. The outcome of the Gallipoli venture, whether defeat or victory, would not matter. The self-doubt had gone. What was the deepest source of self-doubt? The convict stain.

To Ashmead-Bartlett, the most amazing thing he saw on the first Anzac Day was the behaviour of the Australian wounded, which was quite unlike anything he had seen in war before. They were ferried back to the warships and *cheered* on reaching the ships they had left that morning. Even those shot to bits and without hope of recovery cheered. He sensed the reason: 'They were happy because they knew that they had been tried for the first time and had not been found wanting.'

A NATION IS BORN

Ellis Ashmead-Bartlett's account of the Gallipoli landing

The Australians, who were about to go into action for the first time in trying circumstances, were cheerful, quiet and confident. There was no sign of nerve nor of excitement. As the moon waned, the boats were swung out, the Australians received their last instructions, and men who six months ago had been living peaceful civilian lives had begun to disembark on a strange and unknown shore in a strange land to attack an enemy of a different race.

The boats had almost reached the beach, when a party of Turks, entrenched ashore, opened a terrible fusillade with rifles and a Maxim. Fortunately, the majority of bullets went high. The Australians rose to the occasion. Not waiting for orders, or for the boats to reach the shore, they sprang into the sea, and, forming a sort of rough line, rushed at the enemy's trenches. Their magazines were not charged, so they just went in with cold steel.

It was over in a minute. The Turks in the first trench were either bayoneted or they ran away, and their Maxim was captured.

Then the Australians found themselves facing an almost perpendicular cliff of loose sandstone, covered with thick shrubbery. Somewhere, half way up, the enemy had a second trench, strongly held, from which they poured a terrible fire on the troops below and the boats pulling back to the destroyers for the second landing party.

Here was a tough proposition to tackle in the darkness, but those colonials, practical above all else, went about it in a practical way. They stopped for a few minutes to pull themselves together, got rid of their packs, and charged their magazines. Then this race of athletes proceeded to scale the cliffs without responding to the enemy's fire. They lost some men but did not worry. In less than a quarter of an hour the Turks were out of their second position, either bayoneted or fleeing.

But then the Australians, whose blood was up, instead

of entrenching rushed northwards and eastwards search-
ing for fresh enemies to bayonet. It was difficult country to
entrench. Therefore they preferred to advance.

There has been no finer feat in this war than this sudden
landing in the dark and storming the heights, above all
holding on whilst the reinforcements were landing.

These raw colonial troops in these desperate hours
proved worthy to fight side by side with the heroes of Mons,
the Aisne, Ypres, and Neuve Chapelle.

New Zealanders landed with the Australians but were not in
the first wave at dawn on 25 April 1915. The feats of their soldiers led to a growth of national consciousness, but no one ever
said that the New Zealand nation was born at Gallipoli. New
Zealand was not so desperate for the world's approval. Though
a British colony with strong connections to her neighbours in
Australia, she had declined to join them in the Commonwealth
in 1901, often giving spurious reasons for doing so because one
of the strongest reasons could not, without giving offence, be
mentioned: she did not want to join the déclassé Australians
and be identified with their shame.

As the war progressed, the Australian soldiers became
more proficient, and they played a large part in the final battles against Germany on the Western Front. The soldiers had
cemented Australia's reputation before the world, and Australians then had to accept their soldier, warts and all. As warrior for
the empire, respectable people could be proud of him; however,

there were other aspects of his character—his refusal to show respect to officers, his tendency to larrikinism—which were harder to swallow but had now to be indulged. They became willy-nilly acceptable national characteristics because they were characteristics of the digger. Every Anzac Day both parts of the character were on display: the warrior in the formal celebrations in the morning; the drunk and two-up player in the afternoon, when the police turned a blind eye so that the digger as larrikin could have free rein.

This is not Ward's account of how an anti-authoritarian attitude was accepted or tolerated by the nation at large. He claims that the attitude came from the outback workers and in the 1890s spread to the rest of the population, chiefly through the nationalist literature of Paterson and Lawson. In the long term this literature did have an influence, but there were many people around 1900 who were not yet ready to embrace a shearer or a swagman as an iconic national figure. The bourgeoisie was more immediately and completely won over by the digger because he had suddenly made the nation and themselves respectable.

Ward explains that the nationalist literature had tidied up and ennobled the outback worker. The same thing happened to the larrikin. As the real larrikins were becoming less of a menace, C. J. Dennis published *The Sentimental Bloke*, a series of verses about a larrikin who puts behind him the loutish behaviour of his push after he is smitten with love for Doreen. The book was an instant popular success when it was published in 1915. The larrikin had already been redeemed by love when

his deeds in war put him in the pantheon. But the larrikinism still had a hard edge. Australian soldiers trashed and burnt
the red-light district of Cairo, the Wazzir, before they left for
Gallipoli. Dennis defended them in verse in which he depicted
them as innocents who had come from the 'cleanest' land on
earth, a claim that should not surprise.

It wus part their native carelessness, an' part their native skite;
Fer they kids themselves they know the Devil well,
'Avin' met 'im, kind uv casu'l, on some wild Australian night—
Wine an' women at a secon'-rate 'otel.
But the Devil uv Australia 'e's a little woolly sheep
To the devils wot the desert children keep.

So they mooches round the drink-shops,
an' the Wazzir took their eye,
An' they found old Pharoah's daughters pleasin' Janes;
An' they wouldn't be Australian 'less they give the game a fly ...
An' Egyp' smiled an' totted up 'is gains.
'E doped their drinks, an' breathed on them 'is aged evil breath ...
An' more than one woke up to long fer death.

When they wandered frum the newest
an' the cleanest land on earth,
An' the filth uv ages met 'em, it wus 'ard.
Fer there may be sin an' sorrer in the country uv their birth;
But the dirt uv cenchuries ain't in the yard.

They wus children, playin' wiv an asp, an' never fearin' it,
An' they took it very sore when they wus bit ...

'Ave yeh seen a crowd uv fellers takin' chances on a game,
Crackin' 'ardy while they thought it on the square?
'Ave yeh 'eard their 'owl uv anguish
whey they tumbled to the same,
'Avin' found they wus the victims uv a snare?
It was jist that sort uv anger when they fell to Egyp's stunt;
An', remember, they wus trainin' fer the front.

Training for the front was the best of excuses but for a time the censor blocked publication of these verses. They did appear later in the war after the soldiers at the front had made the nation proud.

It was always something of a puzzle to observers of Australia to explain the high standing of working men and the prevalence of their values in the culture. The easy answer was to say the middle class was numerically weak. But in a capitalist society their values should be predominant whatever their numbers. So was it that they lacked the will to rule? I have suggested here that convict origins help to explain this puzzle. The bourgeoisie, sharing the shame of their nation, looked for respectability through 'White Australia' and military prowess, and the forms these took had a strong proletarian cast: the workingman was elevated by the one and was the most notable embodiment of the other.

Australia has now emerged from the long era of repression about its origins. But it is still a distinctive nation because Australians are now *proud* of their convict ancestry. To find a convict ancestor is no longer a matter of shame but for celebration. This is a puzzle to the world at large, who think that slurs about ancestry will still hurt—witness the 'Barmy Army' of English supporters at the cricket who chant: 'You all come from a convict colony, a convict colony…' Suppressed or embraced, convict origins must have an effect. At the very least, a nation pleased about its convict ancestry cannot take itself too seriously.

Those who think that national character is an unnecessary, oppressive and dangerous contrivance will have found this whole discussion otiose. If you are tired of this old theme, read the poet Les Murray's treatment of it in 'Some Religious Stuff I Know About Australia' (in *The Quality of Sprawl*). Religion? And Australian national character? Yes. Murray suggests: 'The ability to laugh at venerated things, and at awesome and deadly things may, in time, prove to be one of Australia's great gifts to mankind. It is, at bottom, a spiritual laughter, a mirth that puts tragedy, futility and vanity alike in their place.'

Murray finds the origins of this spiritual laughter in the underground traditions of working people's irony, of the poor who came to Australia from the old world. In line with the suggestions I have made above, he calls Australia a 'proletarian evolution'. But how does working-class irony become and remain a national attitude? It can happen in a nation which knows itself to be an oddity from the start.

WHY WAS THE POSTWAR MIGRATION PROGRAMME A SUCCESS?

MOST SOCIAL SCIENTISTS IN AUSTRALIAN universities are left-leaning in their politics and so they highlight the inequalities and oppressions of Australian society. When they came to study migrants in modern Australia, they thought they had an easy task. They would show that migrants were marginalised and disadvantaged, which would be another demonstration of the flaws in our society. I am left-leaning myself on some issues, but I recognise that the task in dealing with the great migration programme is to explain its success.

It was easy to describe failure if you accepted the test set by Professor John Western in his textbook on social inequality in Australia. He thought the Italians and Greeks, the first non-Britishers to arrive in large numbers, had suffered 'economic deprivation' because very few had made it into white-collar jobs, and none into the professions and boardrooms. How southern European peasants without English were to get the top jobs in their own lifetimes he did not explain. This first generation actually did very well, even though they were mostly in manual work. They were more likely to own their own homes and keep their children at school and less likely to be unemployed than old Australians. Their children and grandchildren have done exceptionally well: they are now spread through the white-collar jobs and the professions in their proper proportions. Professor Western's equality test has been met—once we avoid the stupidity of applying it to the first generation.

The Italians and Greeks are now also integrated socially. They live not in enclaves, as they did on first arrival, but are spread right through the suburbs. They intermarry at a high rate with other migrants and old Australians. This broadly has been the pattern of all subsequent arrivals, except the Muslim Lebanese. The number of migrants arriving has been so large and intermarriage so common that old Australians have long since ceased to be the largest group in this society. The largest group is the mixture made up from intermarriage between migrants and old Australians.

Of course, there has been some communal tension and racist hostility; it would be silly to assume that there could be none. One way to avoid this is to keep the population homogenous and not have a migration programme. Most countries do not have a migration programme. Australia set itself a severe test of its tolerance by running a programme which has resulted in its having the highest proportion of its people born outside the country of all nations on earth except Israel. Recently, three migration experts, Andrew Markus, James Jupp and Peter McDonald, reported that Australians have a high level of tolerance compared with other peoples. Only a small proportion of people are actively intolerant towards migrants. There is also only a small proportion at the other end of the spectrum, those who are positively tolerant and want the government to support the maintenance of migrant cultures. The authors appear to regret the smallness of this last category—to me, it is another indication of social health.

The transformation in Australian society is the more amazing, given how Australians thought of themselves when the migration programme began in 1945. They were a British people—more British than the British—and proud of their racist policy, a White Australia, and extremely watchful of any threat to it. Twenty years after the programme began, the White Australia policy was dropped. After thirty years, the migration programme accepted people of all races without discrimination. Australia made these changes confidently because it had found that in the absorption of migrants it was an expert.

Jock Collins is a left-leaning professor who does accept the success of the migration programme. In his textbook he calls it 'one of the most successful migration experiences in history'. However, he refuses to give any credit to Australia and Australians for this result. He rejects the explanation that migrants were better accepted in Australia because it is an egalitarian and class-less society. Nonsense, he says. It is as much a class society as any other. The credit must be given to the migrants themselves! But if the migrants are the key factor, why wasn't the same success the result everywhere? These social scientists are unhinged by success. Of course, it is in the nature of Australian society that we will begin to find explanations of the success.

*

Australia is now a multicultural society, but we must not make the common mistake of thinking it was a uniform society before the migration programme began. Old Australia was sharply divided by religion and ethnicity. Coping with differ-ence and ensuring social peace: these were preoccupations of Australian society as it was being formed.

The founding population of Australia was made up of three peoples: the English, Scots and Irish. They were known in Australia as the people of the three kingdoms. In their home countries they had long been enemies of one another, and only comparatively recently had they been brought together as the United Kingdom. The union between Scotland and England took place in 1707, which created Great Britain. Ireland was annexed to this union in 1801, creating the United Kingdom. Though most of the Irish were Catholic, the Protestant Eng-lish still maintained a Protestant church in Ireland and made

Catholics pay for it. Until 1829 Catholics could not be elected to the parliament in Westminster. Most of the Scots were Protestant, but of a more thoroughgoing sort than the English. Their Presbyterian church had rejected bishops and the popish practice of bowing and kneeling in church. On their union with England, the Scots got a better deal over religion than the Irish: the Presbyterian church remained the established church, with the British monarch at its head. So the King was Anglican in England and Presbyterian in Scotland.

The three peoples were in Australia from the start; it was not a Protestant country to which Catholics were added. The Irish Catholics were a large enough minority to be noticed and to make their presence felt—between one in five and one in four. In the United States the Irish Catholics were latecomers, living in overcrowded tenements in New York and Boston and working for low wages. In New South Wales the Irish had the advantage of having come first, even though most were convicts, and they settled on the land as well as in the towns. In Australia the three peoples lived among one another. There were no ethnic enclaves, as there were in the United States and Canada in both town and country. The novelty of Australia for the English was not simply the gum trees and the heat; it was that you had Irish and Scots neighbours.

To one Irish Catholic rebel, the surprising thing was that the battle he had been involved in at home no longer mattered. He was a convict sent for life for his part in a riot when agents of the Protestant church were seizing goods for non-payment of the church rate. In New South Wales he gained his ticket of leave and was saving money to provide a home for his wife, when she could join him. Caroline Chisholm interviewed this man as part of her survey to highlight the advantages of migrating to Australia. He told her: 'Catholics and Protestants live here quiet. I never saw a fight between a Catholic and a Protestant over religion.' As proof, he said that the character reference he needed to bring out his wife had been signed by both priest and parson. He concluded: 'It is a quiet, comfortable country.'

The old enmities between the three peoples and the passion over the differences between Catholic and Protestant had not disappeared. But the desire to control old-world differences was much stronger than the wish to continue them. Governor Bourke did much to keep the peace with his policy of supporting on the same terms the Anglican, Presbyterian and Catholic churches in his 1836 *Church Act*, discussed in Question 2. Community organisations maintained peace by arranging to have representatives of the three peoples on their governing boards and committees. The Irish representation might be token, but it had to be there. This was the political correctness of our ancestors. So hospitals, libraries, friendly societies and sporting clubs were run for the whole community. The attempt at harmony would sometimes break down and there would be sectarian rows. Beware: Catholics are organising to increase their numbers on the board. Scandal: Protestants are trying to convert orphans or deny priests access to the sick. The way to stop these outbreaks would have been to have separate organisations, which would have brought peace at the cost of polarisation.

The term 'British', when used by Australians of themselves in colonial times, was not nostalgia for the old country. It was the proclamation that the peoples of the three kingdoms were equal sharers in this new community, as the third verse of 'Advance Australia Fair' (1878) avers:

> *From England, Scotia, Erin's isle*
> *Who come our lot to share,*
> *Let all combine with heart and hand*
> *To advance Australia fair.*

In Australia, 'British' included the Irish as well as the English and the Scots. In the United Kingdom, 'British' was not much used. The English used it when they remembered to be polite to the Scots. The Scots used it when they wanted to gain English attention. The Irish certainly did not use it of themselves, and no one in England or Scotland thought of the Irish as British. The Irish in Australia were in two minds about the offer to be included as British. It was harder to accept when the British at home were suppressing Irish demands for independence. It became easier towards the end of the nineteenth century, when liberal governments at Westminster were proposing home rule for Ireland—which would have given the Irish the self-governing powers that the Australian colonists (including the Irish) enjoyed.

The Irish Catholics acquired a grievance when the colonial governments from the 1870s onwards withdrew financial support from their schools. Other denominations were prepared to accept the new system of state schooling, from which religion was excluded in normal school hours, but the Catholic bishops were not. They roused their people to keep their schools going and imported nuns and brothers to staff them. The chief political concern of the Catholic bishops for a hundred years was to overturn the injustice they felt their flock suffered in paying for state schools they could not support and getting nothing for their own. Protestants would never agree to government support for Catholic schools; having given up their own schools, they would not allow the state to finance the popish abomination. 'The state schools in danger' was an effective rallying cry at elections. State aid to Catholic and other private schools was not conceded until 1963, by which time few people cared about the old religious division.

After Catholic children were isolated in their own schools, the bishops drew their people further out of the community by encouraging the development of Catholic hospitals, friendly societies, youth groups and sporting clubs. They became very hostile to Catholics marrying Protestants. By the early twentieth century Catholics and Protestants were beginning to live more apart. Protestants, too, developed a network of social and sporting bodies. They ran a secret anti-Catholic organisation, the Masons, to which the Catholics responded with the Knights of the Southern Cross. These looked after their members in business and employment. A few firms would take only Catholics or only Protestants. Some departments in the civil service were one or the other. But in most workplaces people of the two faiths were mixed together. And still there was no residential segregation. Catholic and state-school children might chant nasty ditties at one another on the way home from their different schools and then play together in the same street.

Sectarian feeling erupted during the First World War. Since the Labor prime minister Billy Hughes could not get his party to agree to conscription for overseas service, he put the question to a referendum. A 'yes' vote, which was confidently expected, would force the party to fall into line. Protestant church leaders to a man supported conscription. One Catholic bishop did; others stayed silent, but Archbishop Daniel Mannix of Melbourne, recently arrived from Ireland, put himself forward as a very public opponent.

Amid all the clamour about the need for reinforcements at the front, Mannix was a cool and witty subversive. The newspapers tell us, he said, that the British are repelling all attacks—and now every last man is needed! Mannix's views on war and conscription were not those of the Catholic people. They did not believe, as he claimed, that the war was an 'ordinary sordid trade war' or that it was a disgrace to put on the King's uniform. They enlisted in the same proportion as other denominations until the end of the war. Nor did they show any strong tendency to vote 'no' to conscription. But the Irish Catholics came to adore Mannix, as Patrick O'Farrell explains, because he was a rebel, an Irishman who spoke up for his own and would not be suppressed.

As Mannix became a Catholic hero, he became a monster in Protestant eyes. Australia had failed to adopt conscription: this test of loyalty to the empire had been flunked and Mannix had been the most effective advocate of the 'no' vote. All the old fears of Irish Catholic disloyalty and treachery had been confirmed. Forty thousand people packed into the Exhibition Building in Melbourne in April 1918 to proclaim their loyalty to King and empire and to denounce Mannix.

The Labor Party split over conscription. Hughes and twenty-five of his parliamentary followers left the party and soon after amalgamated with the Liberals to form the Nationalist Party—which was the 'win the war' party. Throughout these manoeuvres, Hughes remained prime minister. Most of those who left the Labor Party with Hughes were Protestants, which left Labor's parliamentary party much more Catholic. The wider party—the trade unions and the branches—did not split, so Labor was still the party of the workers, whether Catholic or Protestant, though its public face was now much more Catholic, which meant some Protestants would not vote for it. Although most Catholics supported Labor, the party had always set itself against taking sides in the sectarian dispute over schools. It maintained this position after the war, to the great annoyance of the bishops. In 1920 in New South Wales they ran their own party to take Catholic votes from Labor—and signally failed. Catholics, Protestants, free-thinkers and socialists continued to rub along together in that fractious beast, the Australian Labor Party.

The other great institution of the twentieth century, the Returned and Services League, kept all old soldiers together by avoiding any party political or religious alignment. But it could not ignore religion completely because it organised a religious service after the Anzac Day march. This was designed as non-denominational, but even so Catholics were forbidden to attend; the tough line of the Catholic bishops was that their people could attend only Catholic services. The Victorian RSL did not give up—it wanted Protestant and Catholic diggers to worship together. In 1938 it found a formula that Archbishop Mannix would accept. Prayers were silent and the hymn was 'Lead, Kindly Light', a cunning choice, written by a Catholic and not actually mentioning God.

This, then, is some of the evidence of how religious and ethnic differences were disruptive in old Australia—and yet not so disruptive. The commitment to containing old-world disputes or overcoming them was very strong. There had been conflict, accommodation and, at a local level, peace. Australians had a way of being good neighbours despite their differences, which were not argued about but set aside. This was good preparation for interacting with migrants peacefully.

The Australian style of interaction was egalitarian. You will remember that Professor Collins said egalitarianism did not exist in Australia because it was a class society like any other. This is a common mistake among social scientists, who should leave off their measurements of inequality and get out more. Egalitarianism is the way Australians soften the differences of inequality; face-to-face, we treat one another as equals. Giving yourself airs is the cardinal offence. As the English novelist D. H. Lawrence wrote in *Kangaroo* (1923), in Australia some people are *better off*, but no one is taken to be *better* than anyone else.

Today, men of all sorts call each other 'mate'. On the goldfields in the 1850s everyone called each other 'mate', but then all were in rough clothes and working with their hands. When normal distinctions reappeared, 'mate' dropped away. But among men rather than women, treating one another as equals grew. This meant, for the upper classes, not talking down to working men, and for workers, not showing the upper classes any particular respect. This is a difficult matter to track. We know it was well established by the First World War, when Australians soldiers were reluctant to salute their officers, though they were willing enough to obey them if they were competent. The officers were not too disturbed by this, for military discipline gave them the means to secure obedience, had they wanted. In this army many officers had come from the ranks. In the RSL after the war, titles of rank were not used, and on the war memorials officers and men appear without rank in one alphabetical list.

What underpinned this development was the prosperity of Australia. Well-paid workingmen could live better, have more self-respect and be more worthy of respect. Unskilled men did not get much less pay than skilled men. A society with a mass of poor, dirty, smelly people at its base is not going to develop democratic manners.

An accommodating, relaxed, egalitarian style would work well in assimilating migrants—but only, of course, if it were applied to them. What made Australians who had little experience of non-Britishers and a good deal of hostility towards them accept them into their society? The short answer is that the government told them they must.

You think that is unlikely, given the anti-authoritarian nature of the Australian people? Actually, Australians are a very compliant people—witness their acceptance of seatbelt wearing, breathalyser tests, helmet wearing, anti-smoking measures and compulsory voting, in all of which Australia was a pioneer. On compulsory voting, no other English-speaking country wants to follow Australia. I have written on this topic: 'Australians are suspicious of persons in authority, but towards impersonal authority they are very obedient.'

*

The rationale for the migration programme was to boost Australia's population and economy so that it could better defend itself against the 'yellow peril' in the next Pacific war. A nation of 7 million had had a very close call in the Second World War. It looked at one stage as if it would be invaded. The Japanese had advanced over the Owen Stanley Ranges to within forty miles of Port Moresby; they had bombed Darwin, Broome and

Townsville; they'd got midget submarines into Sydney Harbour. Only the Americans had saved Australia.

The first federal minister of immigration and the architect of the new policy was Arthur Calwell. He was a ferocious defender of the White Australia policy. He deported Asians who had taken refuge in Australia during the war even if they had married Australians. His pitch to the Australian people was that the migration programme was needed to protect White Australia. Australians were proud of being British and white. If you want to stay white, said Calwell, you will have to yield a little on being British. There are whites in Europe; they can come as migrants if not enough Britishers can be found.

So the migration programme was part of nation-building and national defence. These were not migrants who arrived uninvited or were reluctantly accepted as an obligation of empire, as West Indians and Pakistanis were received into Britain. These migrants were necessary for national survival, which was a purpose readily understood. The war was a very recent memory. The appeal was not to the benevolence of Australians but to their self-interest, a much more secure basis for policy.

Australians might grumble about migrants but they accepted them more or less and then treated them in the customary way. If they had to be here, they should be given a fair go. Systematic exclusion was not the Australian way—except in regard to Aborigines. As one Jewish refugee reported, 'Jews and refugees were not, in all circles, considered the most desirable and admirable of migrants. Yet Australians disliked making a fuss and being nasty to people more than they disliked Jews and foreigners.' To give Professor Collins his due, he makes the same point: Australians might be opposed to migrants but this attitude was not translated into action.

As old Australians got to know migrants, they found grounds for respecting them. My mother, coming home from the city after selling badges for the Mothers and Babies, said migrants never bought a badge but they do dress their children beautifully. My French teacher said Australians stop working when it rains, but the migrants put a bag over their head and shoulders and keep working. My aunt and uncle, living in a very good suburb, admired their Italian neighbour, who had made his fortune out of terrazzo.

Calwell knew Australians' penchant for devising derogatory names for foreigners. He told them that the new migrants had to be called 'New Australians'. They were not guest workers but future citizens. The term is now criticised as assimilationist (the migrants might well not have wanted instantly to be Australians), but it was welcoming and amazingly so. How many other countries would bestow their name immediately on foreigners? New Japanese? New Germans? New French? New Americans? (The Americans preferred hyphens: Polish-Americans, Irish-Americans and so on.) New Britons? Maybe if they came from the empire, but if 10,000 Italians landed at Dover they would not be called New English.

Australians had a double identity: they were Australians and Britons. Migrants could not have been labelled New Britons, since they were not of the right breed. Among other things, they did not know the words of 'Rule Britannia' and must be strangers to the feelings it evoked. But migrants were given half of the double identity, the Australian half, which was the informal, social half: mixing in, being a good bloke, not making a fuss. Paradoxically, the migrant New Australians were invited to be the first pure Australians.

How the new migration programme was implemented will disappoint those who want politicians to keep their promises and proper governance procedures to be followed. Calwell himself was relaxed about including non-Britishers in the migrant intake. He was an admirer of the American 'mixing bowl', which took in people of many nationalities. They had been on show in GI uniforms on the streets of Australia during the war. Calwell, whose grandfather had come from the United States to dig for gold in the 1850s, was very interested in American history. Yet he proceeded cautiously, promising that for every European in the intake there would be ten Britons.

When Calwell travelled to Europe in 1947 to begin recruiting migrants, he immediately struck difficulties. There was no shipping available to carry British migrants to Australia. He had to look to Europe. He began with the people of the fairest skins, the Scandinavians, but they were not interested in migration. The people who *were* interested in migration and for whom the International Refugee Organisation would organise shipping were the Displaced Persons, the people outside their own countries at the end of the war who could not or did not want to return home. Calwell could get any number of them, but taking them would break his promise of ten Britons for every one European. He decided to break it. He got the all-clear from the prime minister, Ben Chifley. The matter was not taken to cabinet for the very good reason it would have been defeated. The British did come later, when ships were available, but in the first four years of the programme they composed only forty per cent of the intake.

The rule of the Refugee Organisation was that countries should not discriminate in their choosing of Displaced Persons. Calwell told his immigration agents to ignore this and to choose the young, healthy and fair-skinned. He then returned to Australia to oversee a public-relations campaign to sell the migration programme to the Australian people. This was the first campaign of its kind, run on American lines, targeting key opinion-makers and interest groups as well as radio and newspapers. The first ship to arrive was a triumph for Calwell's methods—it was a cargo of Balts (people from the Baltic states), single and fair-skinned, the men handsome, the women beautiful, all photogenic (which could not be said of the minister of immigration who welcomed them).

The Displaced Persons who came to Australia were Latvians and Estonians (the Balts), Poles, Ukrainians, Hungarians, Czechs and Yugoslavs, 170,000 in all, a startlingly new element in British Australia. These victims of war were never depicted as people who had suffered much and needed a new home; they were to be welcomed because they were useful.

Calwell ceased being minister of immigration when the Chifley government lost office in 1949. The Liberal government of Robert Menzies carried on the programme, always giving credit to Calwell as its instigator, and it was the Liberals who extended it to include Italians and Greeks, swarthier Europeans, and then Turks. Calwell became leader of the Labor Party and leader of the opposition in 1960. After losing three elections, he yielded his place to Gough Whitlam in 1967. In his last years, he was mortified by his own party's decision to abandon the White Australia policy and the extension of the migration scheme to Asians. He was disappointed never to have been prime minister, but in successfully launching the great migration programme, he made himself a man of more consequence in Australian history than most of its prime ministers.

*

The economic slump that was expected after the end of the Second World War did not eventuate. The economy boomed and there was full employment. When Chifley left office in 1949 there were only 1200 people on the dole. The new migrants readily found work, and the argument that migrants would take jobs from Australians had no force.

The trade unions had always opposed immigration. They were the leading campaigners against Chinese immigration, which had been banned completely, but they were also opposed to government schemes to bring migrants from Britain. As we have seen, working-class opposition to migration was effective in keeping wages high. Calwell gave most attention to the unions in shoring up support for his scheme. He had to persuade them not merely to abandon their suspicion of immigration but also to support a massive inflow of people. Calwell had the advantage of being a staunch Labor man in a Labor government, not someone who could be suspected of wanting to undermine wages and conditions. A Liberal government almost certainly could not have succeeded with the unions.

The need to strengthen White Australia was a good card to play with the unions, but Calwell also had to guarantee that migrants would be paid award wages. This was readily achieved in an economy where wages were controlled by the Commonwealth Arbitration Court and by similar bodies in the states. The unions had always feared that people coming from poorer countries would be prepared to work for lower wages. But once wages were officially controlled, migrants got the going rate, no matter what their experience and expectations. Calwell also had to promise the unions that migrants would be encouraged to join them.

The first wave of migrants, the Displaced Persons, were directed where they should work for a period of two years. They signed up to this as a condition of getting a passage to Australia. This reduced the chance that they would be competing with locals. They were assigned to construction sites in the country and to the Snowy Mountains scheme. Australia got the benefit of their labour, while the men suffered by separation from their families and having their skills ignored. This left some lasting resentment, though most thought it was a fair trade to get the benefits of living in Australia. The peace and the prosperity were very welcome.

The Italians and Greeks who arrived in the 1950s were not directed where to work. They had peasant skills for which there was little demand but they had no trouble finding work in factories, for manufacturing was expanding. So the day after he landed, an illiterate peasant with no English was at work on a production line at award wages and, though he probably did not know it, had joined the union.

With full employment and wages rising rapidly, an Italian or Greek family could do well. Husband and wife were both at work, and after sharing houses for a time families had enough to pay a deposit on their own, so becoming proper suburban Australians. Not altogether so, for to them soil was not to be wasted on flowerbeds or lawn; the land at the front as well as the back of their houses was given over to vegetables and fruit.

Peasants without skills and the English language could no longer do well in Australia. From the 1970s, manufacturing went into decline and generally there was less work for the unskilled. The migration programme moved to acquiring people with skills and the English language. The Liberal government of John Howard that took office in 1996 cut back on the family reunion element of the migration programme, since the people sponsored often did not have the skills to get work (though they might be used by the machine men of the Labor Party to stack branches). A migrant underclass surviving on welfare would have been a sorry end to the success of the 1940s and 1950s.

'Success' may be beginning to pall. The whole story has to acknowledge that some migrants experienced open hostility, that some were disappointed and went home. The disappointment might have many causes, among them that Australia did not reproduce European village life. Migration is always more or less traumatic. The success I am attempting to explain is the absorption of a huge number of outsiders with very little social tension.

*

When the migration programme began, the official policy was that migrants should mix in with the rest of the community, not parade their differences, and assimilate as rapidly as possible to the 'Australian way of life'. In the 1960s the policy was modified from 'assimilation' to 'integration', which still sought social cohesion but more gently. In the 1970s policy was switched fundamentally to accepting a multicultural society, celebrating difference instead of being concerned by it.

Far too much attention is given to policy and its changes in the history of migration. What happened on the ground does not relate closely to policy. You would be closer to the truth if you assumed that developments on the ground were the opposite of policy.

Policy-makers in the 1940s did not want enclaves. They got enclaves, Little Italys and Greek quarters in the capital cities. The migrants did not lose themselves; naturally enough, they stayed together for support in a foreign land. They lived close to one another, they ran their own businesses employing their own people, their restaurants cooked their own food, they published their own newspapers, they played soccer in ethnic teams. Many were slow to accept the invitation to become citizens, which the immigration department took as the test of assimilation. The migrants were living in a free society and simply ignored policy.

Most worryingly of all, the migrants formed national associations, which policy-makers feared would revive old-world divisions. They were in fact chiefly social groups that provided contacts and entertainment. Once the policy-makers realised their mistake, they started funding these associations and so turned them into lobbyists and welfare agencies—even while assimilation remained the official policy.

As migrants prospered, they moved out of the enclaves, and by the second or third generation they had intermarried into another migrant group or with Old Australians. When in the 1970s multicultural policy was proclaimed, encouraging migrants to maintain their culture, the Czechs and Dutch, who had a high rate of 'out' marriage, had almost ceased to exist. The Italians and Greeks were in the process of fading away as a separate group. If the children retained their parents' language, they used it only to speak with their parents; to one another they spoke English. Most of the children were marrying out.

How far migrants remain separate and how far they integrate relates not to government policy but chiefly to the length of time they have been in Australia. The most recent arrivals will be more separate. The second variable is how firmly the groups hold on to their own culture: the Greeks did so more than the Italians, since they had their own church and were more concerned to maintain their language. But the end point has been the same. The attachment of Muslims to their religion may well keep them more separate, though the nature and strength of that attachment varies greatly.

Multiculturalism speaks of different ethnic groups living together and maintaining their cultures. Those who worry that this will create too much diversity and threaten social cohesion don't have to worry too much, since the ethnic groups are disappearing. Australia is much more melting pot than multicultural. Diversity is declining rather than increasing. The demographer Charles Price summed up the Australian experience this way:

> The ethnic character of the Australian population is *not* one where separate ethnic peoples live side by side with relatively little social intercourse, constantly perpetuating their own languages and cultures and keeping distinct by continual marriage within the group.

The following diagram contrasts the impression policy gives with the reality on the ground:

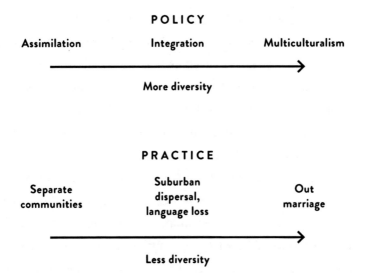

The policies that have had an influence have been unchanging. The programme has been fully controlled by the government, which has monitored its effects and adjusted numbers according to the state of the economy and public opinion. The numbers arriving have been large, but fears that the country is being flooded have mostly been kept under control (with refugees it has been different). For its first thirty years, the programme had bipartisan political support, so that the natural misgivings about a huge influx of foreigners were not exploited for political ends.

Migrants have been drawn from many sources. At first this was to maximise the intake—get the best of the Displaced Persons, whatever their nationality—but later it was a conscious policy designed to 'divide and rule', as it were. If all the migrants had spoken the one language, they would have been better placed to make separatist claims (as the Latinos have in the United States). With a diverse migrant population speaking different languages, only English could be the official language. The running of English classes for migrants at no cost to the students has also been a constant.

The disadvantage of drawing migrants from many countries was that old-world enmities were imported. Serbs and Croats, Greeks and Macedonians, Greeks and Turks, Arabs and Jews: both sides of these conflicts were now resident in Australia, and sometimes old battles were renewed here. Soccer matches were war by other means. Whenever rival migrant groups disturbed the social peace, officialdom came down heavily on them. In the time of assimilation they were condemned for threatening the Australian way of life. More recently they were condemned for threatening multicultural Australia. The message was the same.

The desire to avoid old-world conflicts is more than a policy position; it is deep-seated in the Australian people, evident almost from the time European settlement began. Not high principles, but a quiet life of decent comfort has been the Australian choice. That was bland and passionless in the eyes of many migrants, but they too benefited from the social peace.

*

In the mid-1970s unauthorised migrants began to arrive. These were the boat people, asylum seekers fleeing Vietnam after the communist victory there. This breaching of Australia's borders caused widespread dismay. To his credit, the Liberal prime minister, Malcolm Fraser, accepted the obligation to take Vietnamese refugees, since Australia had supported South Vietnam against the communist North. These were the people Australians—and Americans—had failed to protect. But Fraser moved quickly to stop the arrival of boats. Australian officials processed the refugees in camps in Malaysia and Thailand, and those who were accepted were flown to Australia. Only a little over 2000 people came by boat unofficially; some 79,000 came by plane officially. This marked the beginning of large-scale immigration from Asia.

From the 1990s asylum seekers from the Middle East began to arrive by boat from Indonesia, paying large amounts to 'people smugglers' for the short trip to Christmas Island. The numbers were not large, but most Australians, including recent migrants who had come in the authorised way, wanted this route to Australia closed down. Governments of both sides took ever harsher measures against the boat people in an effort to deter other arrivals, placing them in remote detention centres, processing them at detention centres in New Guinea and Nauru, and denying them any claim to live in Australia even if their refugee applications were successful. The Liberal government of John Howard (1996–2007) did manage to stop the boats; Labor under Kevin Rudd and Julia Gillard (2007–13) at first relaxed the restrictions, but when the number of arrivals rose sharply they had to backtrack. In 2013 the Liberal government of Tony Abbott came to power promising to stop the boats.

The asylum seekers had influential advocates. They were dismayed and ashamed by how Australians treated the boat people. The only explanation they could find was that the Australian people were still deeply racist and xenophobic. It was an unlikely hypothesis, since the Australian people have quietly accepted huge numbers of migrants of every colour and creed. The international comparison of attitudes to migrants, cited above, found Australians very tolerant. While John Howard was stopping the boats, he was accepting into the refugee quota people from Somalia, Muslim and jet-black, who came by air from African camps. Surveys of opinion showed that Australians accepted refugees admitted as part of the government's humanitarian programme; they opposed those who came by boat.

It was the boat people's mode of arrival that caused resentment. It was uncontrolled, so there was the potential for the numbers to blow out. The people were not fleeing immediate danger; they were imposing themselves on the country rather than being invited; and there were grounds for thinking that they were not all genuine refugees. This was a complete reversal of how migration was usually conducted. It affronted the Australian egalitarian instinct, one of the reasons for the migration programme's success. The most telling criticism of the boat people was that they were queue jumpers.

WHY IS AUSTRALIA
NOT A REPUBLIC?

T HIS WAS A QUESTION PUT TO ME BY A YOUNG person who was genuinely puzzled as to why Australia had not become a republic long since.

The short answer is that Australia is not a republic for the same reason that Canada and New Zealand are not. These three became nations within an empire that was unique in history. Britain allowed British settlers overseas the right to self-government in internal affairs, and then in the 1920s full nationhood, with powers over defence and foreign policy. They still shared the same monarch as head of state, but for Canadian purposes the King became the King of Canada, for Australian purposes the King of Australia, and so on. The monarchy was split in order to accommodate independent states within the empire. Of course, the person of the monarch was not split. The King or Queen wore a number of different crowns.

The corollary to this amazing development was that the nations that retained the British monarch as their head of state had to be given a voice in the rules of succession to the throne. In 2011, when the British prime minister proposed to change the rules so that boys would no longer take precedence over girls, he had to seek the agreement of, among others, Canada, Australia and New Zealand.

It is not so surprising that these arrangements, which provided for a loose association of independent nations that shared a common heritage, have survived.

The longer answer to the question is more complicated. Australia has its particular place in the world and its distinctive history with the empire. It produced a separatist and republican movement in the 1880s, but the nation was formed within the empire in 1901, when enthusiasm for empire was running high; it took no part in securing autonomy for the dominions in the 1920s; and in the 1990s it attempted and failed to become a republic. As we shall see, the first two developments relate to the third.

*

In the 1860s and 1870s politicians and leading citizens could proclaim without controversy that Australia's future lay in independence from Britain. The break would be friendly; not immediate, of course, but if Australia continued to grow and prosper, it would have the capacity to look after itself, and any subordination to a mother country would be inappropriate and unnecessary. The North American colonies numbered only 3 million people when they broke from Britain; Australia's population hit 2 million in 1877.

When the American colonies declared their independence from Britain they needed the military assistance of another great power, France, to win their war of independence. When Australians thought of a peaceful break with Britain, they were assuming that Australia was safe in the South Pacific, far from the rivalries of the great European powers. She had a natural defensive barrier, being, as 'Advance Australia Fair' proclaimed, 'girt by sea'.

In the 1880s there was a rude disruption to this dreaming. Bismarck, the German chancellor, decided that the German Empire was not to be a land empire only; it would match Britain by acquiring colonies overseas. He looked to the Pacific for unclaimed territory. France, Germany's sworn enemy, followed suit. So Australia, before it was a nation, was cast into the arena of imperial conflict.

Only one power could stop these potentially hostile empires: Great Britain. Australia's first attempt at federation, in 1883, was prompted by the desire to put more pressure on Britain to make these upstarts clear off. It was initiated by Victoria, which made New South Wales suspicious, which made Victoria more determined to succeed: Britain might ignore six squabbling colonies;

it could not ignore a nation. But Victoria had to settle for a weak Federal Council, which New South Wales did not join.

It took three years before this enfeebled council held its first meeting. Meanwhile, the campaign to get Britain to protect the colonies continued. Thomas McIlwraith, the premier of Queensland, suspecting that Bismarck was eyeing off New Guinea, sent the police magistrate at Thursday Island to Port Moresby to claim this territory for Britain. The British government disowned the move, which enraged the Australians, who were convinced Britain was ignoring them. The feeling intensified when Bismarck did then claim the island. But Germany took only the north-eastern segment; by agreement between the two powers, Britain claimed the south-east (the western half was held by the Dutch).

The French were eyeing off the New Hebrides (now Vanuatu) and planning to send convicts there. This touched a raw nerve in Australia: *You think we won't mind because convicts have been here before?* They did mind, deeply, that their own past was being thrown in their faces. On convicts, the British government got the message. It organised with the French to stop the convict plan, and in return allowed France to claim the islands. But those tetchy Australians were not satisfied: they wanted Britain to stop the French altogether.

The British were more attentive to demands from Australia's colonies than their politicians gave them credit for. The Australians had no sense of what a delicate business it was for Britain to keep the peace among the powers while they carved up the world and to protect its empire. The Australians were fixed in their view that Britain did not take them seriously because they were colonials. All this would change if they could become leaders of a nation.

In Britain itself there was a new awareness of the usefulness of the colonies. Germany and the United States were overtaking Britain in economic strength and threatening its pre-eminence in the world. If Britain were to keep its position, it would need to recruit the economic and military power of its colonies.

An Imperial Federation League was formed in London in 1884, with a high-profile membership, to promote a formal union between the mother country and its self-governing colonies. In 1887 the British government held the first Colonial Conference, which brought together in London the leaders of all the self-governing colonies. They were briefed on the matters that concerned them. All the premiers who would accept knighthoods received them. The Australians agreed that in order to increase the strength of the British navy in Australian waters, they would contribute to its cost. The conference was the making of Alfred Deakin, the native-born leader of the Victorian delegates, who refused a knighthood and was most outspoken in his criticism of the British prime minister, Lord Salisbury. Deakin said the Australians had not come across the world to be told that there were difficulties in dealing with the French. The colonies expected the British to care more for their interests and to take it up to the French.

A growing British interest in the colonies was reassuring as dangers loomed—and also threatening. Instead of Australia evolving naturally to independence, something very different was happening. A nation of great distinction was in the offing—pure, young and free—and now it was to be tied more firmly to the old world. Would membership of the empire assist the new nation or corrupt it? Would the new nation serve British interests rather than Australian? A nation within an empire could still appear as a contradiction in terms. Some thought that forming a nation must threaten loyalty to the empire, others that a nation within an empire could be no true nation.

The puzzled and the doubtful were not an insignificant force. Thomas McIlwraith was out of parliament by the time of the Colonial Conference. When Samuel Griffith, the Queensland premier, returned from London with the undertaking to help pay for the British navy, McIlwraith's supporters successfully moved in the parliament to reject it. McIlwraith organised his followers into a National Party and won the 1888 election with a programme of an independent federation of Australia. McIlwraith was not opposed to some connection to Britain but wanted Australia to keep its distance. 'Alliance not dependence' was his slogan.

There were now, in the mid-1880s, a small group of outright republicans who were active in Queensland and New South Wales. They were chiefly newly arrived workingmen from Britain, for these two colonies were maintaining an immigration programme. These men brought their republicanism and socialism with them from Britain. They were not republicans because they were thoroughgoing Australian nationalists (they were, after all, fresh off the boat) but because they saw the monarchy as an entrenchment of privilege and inequality.

The racy national newspaper the *Bulletin*, published in Sydney from 1880, was republican. It, too, took its bearings from the new radical agenda in Britain, but gave it an Australian bite and wit. It was the only newspaper with cartoons, which were vivid, sharp and devastating. The *Bulletin* fostered a national literature, publishing the first works of Henry Lawson and A. B. 'Banjo' Paterson. Respectable people shunned it because it was rude about the royal family.

Republicanism now caused offence: it was radical, disrespectful—and dangerous if it gave Britain the idea that the colonies did not want its assistance. Its outright adherents were few, but behind the hostile response to them was a fear that their influence might grow, given the uncertainty about the nation (not yet formed), the empire (now perhaps too interested in colonies), and how the relation between the two might work. Republicanism was an option, and until recently an uncontroversial one.

The republicans of Sydney grabbed the limelight in 1887, when they opposed plans to celebrate Queen Victoria's golden jubilee. They took over a public meeting at the town hall that was organising a treat for schoolchildren, and resolved that a picnic in honour of the Queen was a threat to democratic values. A second meeting was called to counter this disloyalty, but with printed invitations to keep the republicans out. They forged the invitations and swamped this meeting too. With the elite of Sydney on the stage, the republicans kept up such a barrage of hoots and jeers that no speaker could be heard. Three cheers were given for the republic. The picnic was now long forgotten. Sydney had to organise a monster demonstration to show its loyalty to the Queen, which it did in the Exhibition Building, with strict surveillance of those attending and with police and military protection.

Sir Henry Parkes, premier of New South Wales for the fourth time, was on the stage in the town hall when the republicans reduced the meeting to shambles. He led the pack in denouncing their disloyalty. Privately, however, he had some sympathy with the young men who were drawn to this cause. After all, he had briefly been a republican himself in the 1850s, another time of uncertainty about the colony's future, when Britain had not yet conceded the right to self-government.

Parkes agreed to meet one young republican, the native-born budding poet Henry Lawson. The young man's mother, Louisa, a leading advocate of women's suffrage (a cause Parkes supported), hoped Parkes would find him a job. That does not seem to have happened, but Parkes praised his poetry. He may have seen the first poem Lawson published in the *Bulletin*, 'Sons of the South' (1887), or Henry may have taken it to show him:

> *Sons of the South, make choice between*
> *(Sons of the South, choose true)*

The Land of the Morn and the Land of E'en,
The Old Dead Tree and the Young Tree Green,
The land that belongs to the lord and the Queen,
And the land that belongs to you.

Parkes considered that a crisis in Australia's affairs was approaching. If the allure of separatism and republicanism was to be broken, an Australian nation with full powers had to be quickly created, and Britain had to be persuaded to allow it a voice in the determination of empire policy. Then it would be no derogation for the new nation to remain in the empire. In 1889 he launched his campaign for federation and wrote to Lord Salisbury, the British prime minister, about the need for an Empire Council.

Parkes' campaign was amazingly successful. As we saw in Question 4, he solved the impasse between Victoria and New South Wales over the trade policy of the new nation. By 1891 a federal convention had agreed on a draft constitution for the Commonwealth of Australia. It provided for a nation within the empire, but it was a nation with full powers, including over defence and foreign policy, even though for the moment the British government would have oversight of those matters. The constitution was not adopted but its writing settled many fears. The British government had played no part in its creation; Australians were determining their own future.

Lord Salisbury did not give Parkes a very satisfactory reply. Assuming that Parkes was proposing an imperial parliament (one of the schemes of the Imperial Federation League),

Salisbury said Australia would be swamped in such a body by the representatives of India, a sure-fire scare for White Australia. But Parkes was wanting something different: a council representing all the white settlement colonies, which would set the direction of the empire's defence and foreign polices. He wrote again to set Salisbury right, but this part of his plan now mattered less, though it was to be pursued later by many Australian prime ministers. In the 1890s the wind had gone out of the sails of separatism and republicanism. Depression, strikes and bank failures made Australia a less likely prospect for independent existence, and socialists and republicans were diverting their energies to the new Labor Party, which was toying with socialism but not republicanism. The *Bulletin*, the most powerful advocate of republicanism, abandoned the cause in 1891, and in 1894 accepted federation under the crown.

In the 1890s enthusiasm for empire grew in Britain and Australia. In 1895, as the Australian premiers agreed to the calling of another constitutional convention, in London Joseph Chamberlain became secretary of state for the colonies. He was a vigorous, determined minister, and committed to strengthening the empire. Correctly discerning that the colonies wanted to be more than second-class citizens, he set out to give them honoured roles at the empire's heart. For Queen Victoria's diamond jubilee, in 1897, he brought troops from all round the empire to parade with the Queen on her way to St Paul's Cathedral. All the premiers from the settlement colonies were invited. The proceedings of the second Federal

Convention in Australia had to be suspended to allow the premiers to attend. Chamberlain organised that the colonial premiers would stand with the great British ministers of state on the steps of the cathedral to welcome the Queen.

In 1899 Chamberlain provoked the Boer (Dutch) republics in southern Africa into war. His plan was to amalgamate them, and their newfound wealth in gold and diamonds, into British South Africa. The second part of his plan was to run the war as an imperial venture, with the colonies sending troops. They responded enthusiastically. The bushmen's contingents from Australia brought renown to the new nation by fighting and dying in South Africa. Australian veterans of this war participated in the federation parade in Sydney in 1901.

The parade was organised by William Lyne, the premier of New South Wales, who thought the most exciting thing about the new nation was that it was part of the empire. He proposed that the parade should be a repeat of the imperial military display for the Queen's jubilee in London. Chamberlain, of course, was delighted with Lyne's idea and badgered the British Treasury to pay for it. So the stars of the show on Sydney's streets were the Imperial Life Guards in their shining breastplates and the Indian troops in their turbans. They quite overshadowed the floats that related to Australian federation, like the one organised by the trade unions that carried a young girl dressed in white to represent Australia.

This was an early sign that the civic element in Australian nationalism was going to weaken, a theme we began at the end of Question 4. The enthusiasm for empire, military glory and blood sacrifice was overshadowing the civic achievement of uniting six colonies peacefully. Australians would take pride not in making a democratic constitution by democratic means, but in the exploits of their sportsmen and the superiority of their soldiers. The pure young woman as symbol of Australia went into a decline.

The Australian nation was always going to be British. Being British was a means of uniting the people of the three kingdoms of England, Scotland and Ireland. Part of Parkes' appeal for union was that people of the one blood should not remain apart: 'the crimson thread of kinship' ran through them all. But by 1901 the nation was something more: indisputably part of the British Empire. To speak of republicanism was now taboo.

It happened that Australian nationalism strengthened at the same time as enthusiasm for empire grew. The two reinforced each other. The nation was more glorious and more secure by being part of the empire; the empire was stronger and more benign by incorporating a nation rather than having to supervise six quarrelsome colonies.

Loyalty to empire did not mean subordination. In 1900 Alfred Deakin described his countrymen as 'independent Australian Britons'. The independence was insisted on. In the early 1900s Britain wanted Australia to give some undertaking that it would join the looming war in Europe; it refused, reserving the right to make a judgement when and if the war came. Between the wars, there were heated disputes between Australia and Britain over trade policy.

The disagreements between Australian and British ministers were usually kept inside the family, so that even their own people did not know about them. It was only with the opening of the archives that we learnt how furious Billy Hughes was when it seemed that Britain, without consultation, had committed Australia to a war against Turkey in 1922 (which did not eventuate), and how cautious Prime Minister Menzies was in 1939 about committing Australian soldiers to a European conflict, despite Britain's urging. Australia always wanted Britain to take more heed of its views, to consult more, to be more loyal to empire, as they put it, but the disappointments were borne because of the benefits that still flowed from the connection.

*

The movement to federate the Australian colonies and the establishment of the Commonwealth coincided with the rise of Japan. In 1895 Japan beat China in war; in 1905 it announced itself as a power to be reckoned with by defeating a European power, Russia. Just a week's sailing to the south, Australia was now confronted with an expansionist Asian power that could well take exception to the immigration policy enshrined as a national ideal, White Australia. Australia could not resist or defeat Japan on its own; it needed the empire's support more than ever.

The problem with relying on empire was that the British navy was now overstretched in dealing with the rise of Germany and could no longer rule all the seven seas. To maintain British power in the Pacific, in 1902 Britain made an alliance with … Japan. This was not altogether reassuring to the Australians. In the years before the First World War, Australia spent heavily on defence, in case the British navy could not reach its shores in time if Japan turned nasty. It created an Australian navy and, in a very un-British move, made training for the army compulsory for young men in peacetime.

The Anglo–Japanese alliance survived up to and during the First World War, in which Japan was a very circumspect ally of Britain. Japanese warships escorted Australian troopships across the Indian Ocean. As Britain asked more and more of the Japanese navy, Japan upped its demands, some of which were to be exacted at the expense of Australia. As Neville Meaney says, while Australia was fighting in the hot war in Europe to help save Britain and the empire, there was 'a cold war' being fought between Japan and Australia.

Although Australia had seized German New Guinea at the opening of the war, Japan claimed its outlying islands that were north of the equator. Britain put pressure on Australia to agree to this demand. When the Australian prime minister, Billy Hughes, was in London in 1916, the Japanese ambassador made two further requests: for a trade treaty and a relaxation of immigration restrictions. On trade something might be done, but Hughes would never agree to relax the White Australia policy.

THE MOTHERLAND'S MISALLIANCE

Britannia: 'Now, my good little son, I've got married again; this is your new father. You must be very fond of him.'

He returned home believing that the gravest threat to Australia was what Japan, Britain's ally, would demand at war's end.

On his return, Hughes announced his support for conscription. His enemies in the Labor Party accused him of having been 'duchessed' in Britain and of now doing Britain's bidding. Actually, the closer he got to British decision-makers, the more worried he was that they might sell out to Japan. He wanted conscription not so much for the war to be won, but so that Australia would be seen to be making an all-out effort in the same way as everyone else. Otherwise, Australia might be in a weaker position at the peace talks.

Because Britain was so hard-pressed in the war and relied so much on troops from the empire, the prime ministers of the self-governing dominions were given places on an imperial war cabinet that sat in London. This was close to the council of empire that Parkes had sought—except that not all important matters were put to it. But it gave Hughes a base from which to insist that the dominions should have their own representatives at the peace conference in Versailles. There, Hughes was the most pugnacious and relentless delegate. He went well armed. Although two referendums on conscription had been lost, Australia had managed—just—to maintain its five divisions in the field, and Australian troops had played a prominent part in the defeat of Germany. Though he came from a small country, Hughes boasted that he spoke for 60,000 dead.

At the conference, Hughes badgered the whole British Empire delegation to support him in protecting White

Australia. He insisted that the White Australia policy must apply to New Guinea, which Australia was to administer under a League of Nations mandate. This was not to turn the brown-skinned natives into whites, but to prevent the Japanese and any other Asians from settling there. Originally, the holders of mandated territories were to allow free access to them; finally, to satisfy Australia (and South Africa and New Zealand, which had also taken over German colonies), a special class of mandate was created which allowed domestic laws of the controlling power to operate within them.

The other threat came from the Japanese, who wanted the founding documents of the League of Nations to include a declaration of racial equality and a requirement that, in all League countries, the people of League members be treated equally. No matter how much this was watered down, Hughes would not have a bar of it; if it meant anything, it was the first step to undo White Australia. The Canadians told him that their immigration arrangement with Japan worked well: in theory, there was the same access as for Europeans, but in practice Japan did not give exit visas to workingmen. The Japanese assured Hughes he could have this deal. Wouldn't that settle his chief worry?

It would not. Fear of cheap labour had been the origin of White Australia but it had morphed into a national item of faith, held with religious fervour. There was something crazy-brave about Hughes on this issue, on which he was the true representative of his country. The nation would die rather than yield on this.

Hughes' objection meant that the Japanese proposal was not adopted in any form. They went away very aggrieved. Hughes got his way only because he had the support of the empire. One of the effects of this connection was that Australia could be offensive to the great Asian power to its north.

On his return, Hughes was greeted as a hero. He told parliament that as a result of his efforts White Australia was safe, and reminded members that Australia was a nation by the grace of God and the British Empire. The country could only be held, he said, because of the British navy. Sadly, the British navy could still not be totally relied on. With the Anglo–Japanese alliance no more, Britain undertook to protect Australia from Japan by building a naval base at Singapore. In time of danger it would send a fleet to operate from this base. Just how many ships? How long would they take to arrive? These were the questions Australian leaders kept asking between the wars. They have been criticised for being so trusting, but they kept asking because they were not reassured. What else could they do? They spent more money on defence, they sought (unsuccessfully) some American guarantee, and they urged Britain to appease Germany and Japan even more fulsomely. It can be that a small power is unable to find a guarantee against a great power. A weaker Britain was much better than nothing.

Between the wars Canada and South Africa sought a formal recognition of their complete powers of nationhood and began to act on them. Canada opened embassies in Paris, Washington and Tokyo; South Africa in Paris, Washington and

The Hague. These dominions were not strategically exposed, as Australia was, and they had large non-British elements in their populations: the French in Quebec and the Afrikaners in the old Boer republics. As Australia boasted, it was ninety-eight per cent British, its trade was overwhelmingly with Britain and it needed the empire for its defence. Hence, Australia took no part in the movement to formalise full nationhood; in fact, it opposed it. Australia assumed that the powers of nationhood existed, but to formalise them would undermine the common feeling that must continue if the empire was still to be a power in the world. Australia's hope was still for some mechanism for binding the empire of self-governing dominions more closely together. Ideally, there should be an empire defence and foreign policy. Canada and South Africa had less need for this and did not want to be bound to what Britain and the empire might do.

The Australian Labor Party was in opposition at the federal level for nearly all the years between the wars. It was isolationist and suspicious of empire, given what loyalty to empire had led to in 1914–18, but it took no interest in the formulation of dominion autonomy. Its support of White Australia was as fervent as ever, which meant any questioning of the empire connection was gesture, not policy.

Arthur Balfour, a British elder statesman, produced for the 1926 Imperial Conference a definition of the new empire. His clever, elegant words omitted the term 'independence' partly in order to placate Australia:

> Great Britain and the Dominions are autonomous Commu-
> nities within the British Empire, equal in status, in no way
> subordinate one to another in any aspect of their domestic
> or external affairs, though united by a common allegiance
> to the Crown, and freely associated as members of the Brit-
> ish Commonwealth of Nations.

These principles were embodied in the *Statute of Westminster* in 1931. By the wish of Australia, the statute was not to apply to Australia until its parliament adopted it. This did not occur until 1942, when, without fanfare, it was adopted to remove doubts about Australia's powers over merchant shipping and security during the war.

*

The war with Japan began on 7 December 1941, just a few weeks after government in a hung parliament passed from the Coalition to Labor, led by John Curtin. Winston Churchill sent not a fleet but two battleships to Singapore to meet the Japanese threat. Sadly, their aircraft-carrier escort was delayed, and the Japanese sank the *Prince of Wales* and the *Repulse* from the air. The naval base had lost its purpose. Churchill considered abandoning it as the Japanese advanced rapidly down the Malay Peninsula. Curtin's government told him this would be an act of betrayal, after all the promises that had been given over Singapore. This was one factor that led Churchill to leave the British and Australian troops there. They could not resist the Japanese advance and 100,000 empire soldiers went into captivity.

As this disaster for the British Empire and Australia unfolded, Curtin addressed the Australian people in a New Year's message on 27 December 1941. He said: 'Without any inhibitions of any kind, I make it quite clear that Australia looks to America, free of any pangs as to our traditional links or kinship with the United Kingdom.' This is the most-quoted statement by an Australian prime minister. It is taken as marking a new era in Australian history. It is a profound mistake to do so.

There was nothing novel in Curtin looking to America. The regular speculation about Australia's likely fate if Britain should fail to protect her was that she would have to look to America and trust that the bonds of blood would be stronger than American isolationism. Robert Menzies, prime minster in the early part of the war, visited Washington on his way home from London and received from President Roosevelt some guarantee of Australia's security if Japan attacked. On his return to Australia in May 1941, he said at a great meeting in the Sydney Town Hall, which was broadcast nationally, 'We in Australia look more and more to the east and those in Britain look more and more to the west to the great democracy of the United States. I believe we shall not look there in vain.' This was greeted with cheers.

If Curtin's appeal was not novel, it could be said to have got a result. The Americans did come, but not because of Curtin's New Year's message. This was a newspaper article written by his press secretary and addressed to the Australian people. At this time Churchill and Roosevelt were meeting in Washington to plan a united global strategy. That America would carry the chief burden of the war in this part of the world had already been decided. There were already American troops in Australia.

The novelty in Curtin's statement was the phrase 'free of any pangs' as to the nation's British connection. This caused great dismay in Australia and annoyed both Churchill and Roosevelt. Curtin withdrew it and proclaimed his loyalty to King and empire, which was his own genuine position: 'There is no part of the Empire more steadfast in loyalty to the British way of living and British institutions than Australia. Our loyalty to His Majesty the King goes to the very core of national life.' He went further: the 'indissolubility of Empire' was the foundation of Labor's war programme! Curtin's chief defence adviser was right: he should have written 'without any lessening of bonds with the United Kingdom'.

Though Australia became the base for the American counterattack against Japan, the United States gave no ongoing guarantee for Australia's security. That was obtained in the ANZUS treaty of 1951, negotiated by the Menzies Liberal government. Over the years, because some elements of the Labor Party have opposed the treaty, Labor has been targeted as being 'soft' on defence. Labor's reply is that Curtin was responsible for originating the American alliance. It is not so.

Actually, by the end of the war Curtin was worried about the claims the United States was staking out in the Pacific, and worked to create a stronger British Empire. He proposed the establishment of a secretariat to coordinate the members' activities between the conferences of prime ministers. Australian prime minsters of all stripes had tried something like this and failed—as did Curtin. Canada did not want it.

Still, Curtin had come to realise that Australia had more chance of influencing Britain than the United States. Britain was still a great power, though now clearly behind the United States and Russia. After Curtin's death in 1945, the Labor government of Ben Chifley maintained close ties with Britain. The rationing of butter was continued to keep Britain supplied. The government allowed Britain to develop a long-range rocket facility at Woomera in South Australia. In the 1950s Britain tested its atomic and nuclear bombs in Australia. Australians welcomed the mushroom clouds because Britain with the bomb made Australia more secure.

With all the changes wrought by the war, Australia was in the 1950s still a British society in all the ways Curtin had outlined. I can testify to that. As a schoolboy, I never heard of Curtin; I did hear of Churchill. At school I learnt British history, geography and poetry. At recess we played a rough game known as British bulldog. On Monday mornings we sang 'God Save the King', and after 1952 'God Save the Queen'. When the Queen visited in 1954, and drew the largest crowds in Australian history, the boys at my school had the honour of performing what were known as 'physical jerks' in front of her. At the Monday-morning ceremony when the Union Jack was raised, we intoned these words:

I am an Australian.
I love my country, the British Empire.
I honour her King, King George the Sixth.
I salute her flag, the Union Jack.
I promise cheerfully to obey her laws.

In my youth the drinking of toasts at all private and public functions was still preceded by the 'loyal toast'. I played a small part in the undoing of this practice in the 1960s. As the MC at a friend's wedding, I omitted the loyal toast and was rebuked by an uncle of the groom.

In the 1960s, British Australia came to an end. This was signalled by Britain itself when it sought membership of the European Community. Of all the ways in which it was envisaged that Australia might depart from Britain, none had Britain abdicating its position as head of the British world. It was the Brits who finally pushed Australians into being only Australians. It no longer made sense to be 'independent Australian Britons'.

*

A 'new nationalism' emerged to replace the gap left by the British abdication. Australia equipped itself with all the panoply of independent nationhood: a national anthem, an oath of allegiance, more support for Australian artistic works, a system of honours, Australian-born governors and governors-general, an end to appeals to the Privy Council. From the 1960s, a few prominent writers and intellectuals called for a republic, a subject no longer taboo but still highly controversial.

The most notable was the historian Manning Clark, the author of the six-volume *History of Australia*, who became a sort of guru to progressive causes in Australia. The last volume of his *History*, published in 1987, was entitled 'The Old Dead Tree and the Young Tree Green', Henry Lawson's words of a hundred years before. Clark wanted a republic to reinvigorate the old radical tradition, to give the nation a new life, which wasn't a remake of Europe or in awe of it. This dream drew some to republicanism but it was not shared by the organised movement for a republic that began in 1991.

The Australian Republican Movement was notable for the narrowness of its aims. It focused solely on the republic, to which no other causes were to be hitched, and the republican changes it sought were minor. The governor-general should be replaced by a president with similar powers (chiefly ceremonial), who would be selected by a two-thirds vote of a joint sitting of parliament.

The movement never had a large membership but was far more influential than its predecessors. The Sydney republicans of the 1880s forged invitations and disrupted meetings. The Australian Republican Movement of 1991 was launched at a five-star Sydney hotel, and since its leaders were so well connected, two policemen of the special branch guarded the door. The movement came from within the new establishment of Sydney, comprising people from business, the professions, media and the arts who were, variously, wealthy, successful and famous. It encouraged branches in other states but only in Sydney was there this galaxy of talent. Immediately it had an effect: public support for the republic rose. Polls found that over fifty per cent of Australians were in favour—in some polls over sixty per cent.

The leaders of the movement were moved chiefly by status concerns. They felt themselves and their nation demeaned by the remaining connection to Britain. It was absurd that a successful, multicultural nation close to Asia should still be shackled to the British monarchy. The nation needed its own identity. They spoke of a nation that was not yet mature, that had not fully left its colonial past behind—a nation not fully realised. It must signal a new beginning by a break from Britain. Not all Australians shared these views, not even all who were willing to support a republic, but they do point to the reasons why a move to a republic had emerged much more strongly in Australia than it was later to do in Canada and New Zealand.

The gap that the republicans sensed in their national history was true enough: Australians had no story of the origin of their polity. The landmark of 1901, the creation of a democratic nation, was eclipsed by the enthusiasm for empire and the symbolic strength of the soldiers who fought for it. The landmark of 1931, the establishment of dominion independence, had been spurned (as it was by New Zealand). The result is that even the High Court cannot say when Australia became an independent nation. Was it in 1931, even though Australia did not adopt the *Statute of Westminster*? But can it be in 1942, when it was adopted, for in 1939 Australia appointed its first ambassadors? The expert authors of *Colony to Reluctant Kingdom* opt for 1931. Canadians have a story of their rise to independent dominion status. They demanded it within the councils of the empire in the 1920s, and in 1982 their constitution, which had been drawn up in Britain in the 1860s, was repatriated to Canada so that it could be amended there.

The absence of civic memory in Australia is highlighted by its national day being no more than the anniversary of the arrival of the British at Sydney Cove in 1788. The federation fathers thought that 1 January would become Commonwealth Day, a true national day, to honour the inauguration of the federation, but after one year that was forgotten and 1 January reverted to being solely New Year's Day. By contrast, Canada's national day celebrates the creation of the Canadian federation in 1867. New Zealand's national day celebrates not the first British settlement but the Treaty of Waitangi, signed in 1840 between the British governor and the Maori chiefs, which is now regarded as the nation's founding document.

Of the three dominions, the composition of Australia's population changed the most in modern times. It used to be ninety-eight per cent British and proudly white (which Canada could not approach because of the French, and New Zealand because of the Maori). Since the 'purity' of Australia's population was under threat from Japan, it had to look to Britain for protection. The fall of Singapore and the advance of the Japanese did not lead to a lessening of the British allegiance, but after the war it did propel the nation to its massive migration programme. In the planning, only ten per cent of the intake was to be non-British, but immediately, as we saw in Question 6, it was much higher than that. The range of source countries widened, and in the 1960s the strategic danger of Australia in Asia led to a reversal of previous policy: the abandonment of White Australia and the encouragement of migration from Asia. After being the most British dominion, Australia had become the most multicultural.

Australia had more to live down in its past than the other dominions. Unlike Canada and New Zealand, it had never made treaties with its indigenous people. Those two dominions also excluded Asian immigration, but without making race central to their national identities. Australia was closest to Asia and had been the most offensive to Asians.

*

Paul Keating, Labor prime minister between 1991 and 1996, was responsible for the first official attempt to transform Australia into a republic. He boasted that the republic was just an 'after-dinner mint' topic until he took it up, which overlooked the initial success of the Australian Republican Movement, which had made republicanism respectable. Keating linked the cause to his grand vision of Australia remade: an open economy, land rights for Aborigines, security in Asia not against it, and, to cap it all, a republic. At the 1993 election he promised that an expert committee would look into options for the republic. The experts, chaired by merchant banker Malcolm Turnbull, the leader of the Australian Republican Movement, duly produced an exhaustive report that came down in favour of a president who would be elected by a joint sitting of parliament on a two-thirds vote.

The visionary republican prime minister was also highly combative: he lambasted the Liberal opposition both for being empire men in the past (as if Labor had never supported empire) and for not supporting the republic now. The republican movement was delighted to have a prime minister committed to its cause, but knew that if it were to succeed, it could only be with bipartisan support. The change would have to be effected by a constitutional referendum, notoriously difficult to carry, and impossible if one of the major parties was opposed.

The Liberals were actually divided on the republic. They criticised Keating for pushing his republic down the people's throats, and promised that, if they won the 1996 election, a constitutional convention would be called to consider the matter. Belatedly, Keating became less partisan. At the 1996 election he promised that the Australian people would vote on whether they wanted a republic; if the answer was yes, a multi-party parliamentary committee would draw up a proposal.

The Liberals won the 1996 election under the leadership of John Howard, an avowed monarchist. It was put to him that, given the fall in support for the monarchy, the proper conservative course was for him to effect the change to a republic in a prudent way. That he was personally opposed to the republic did not free him from that obligation. (Did he not know that the Duke of Wellington did not believe in Catholic emancipation or the reform of parliament, though he was crucial to the passage of both?) The need was more pressing, for opinion polls now revealed that the people much preferred to replace the governor-general with a president directly elected by themselves, a far more disruptive change to the Westminster system of government. Howard was unpersuaded. So the official move to a republic via a convention was presided over by a prime minister opposed to the change.

Half the delegates to the convention were elected by postal ballot, and half were appointed by the government. The appointed included political leaders from the federal and state parliaments and community leaders. About sixty per cent of the vote went to republicans and thirty per cent to monarchists, with the rest indeterminate. To the credit of the government, the balance of opinion among appointed delegates was much the same. There was a clear majority for the republic, and the convention duly voted for a republic in principle. But what sort of republic was it to be?

The republicans were badly split. About forty per cent of the republican vote had gone to supporters of a directly elected president. These were latecomers to the scene, in part funded by the monarchists as a spoiling tactic. To appease them, the plan for parliamentary election of the president was widened to provide for community input on likely presidents before the prime minister chose one to be sent to a joint sitting of the parliament. This scheme just failed to win a majority of the convention delegates, but Howard, confident that it would be defeated, undertook to carry it through the parliament and put it to the people.

At the referendum, held in 1999, the monarchists did not support the Queen. They joined with the direct-electionists to oppose a president approved by the parliament. This was denounced as a politicians' republic—even by politicians. The people should hold out for something better, they said: a president elected by themselves. The monarchists hoped that once this proposal had been killed, there would be no other. The proposal was comfortably defeated: a forty-five per cent 'yes' vote nationally, with no state recording a majority. Half those who voted 'no' were supporters of a republic. A proposal for a directly elected president (which the politicians would not have put) would almost certainly have been carried.

The Australian Republican Movement had opted for a president elected by the parliament because it was determined on success; given the long history of failed constitutional referendums, change should be kept to a minimum. They knew the politicians would not want to create a head of state with a popular mandate who might challenge the authority of a prime minister and so disturb the Westminster system of government. They knew the Australian people did not want a politician for a head of state. The best way to avoid that was to force both the major parties to agree on a candidate: hence the provision for a two-thirds vote in the parliament. If there were an open election, the parties would run candidates and a politician (or someone supported by a political party) would be elected.

Their scheme failed because of the seeming perversity of the people: by preferring the direct election of the president, they would likely get a president who was the opposite of the type they wanted. In old British Australia, an appeal to the principles of the Westminster system of parliamentary government would have carried more weight, but a republic was only being proposed because British Australia was long gone. The common understanding was that because Australia was a democracy, the people should themselves elect the president. A directly elected president was preferred in part because some people wanted to *disturb* the existing system of government. They wanted a president who would 'kick ass' and make politicians keep their promises. Rather than giving Australia a new identity, the Australian Republican Movement had provided the opportunity for a populist revolt.

So the last part of the answer to the question of why Australia is not a republic is that at the moment when republicanism seemed possible, the growing distrust of politicians meant that politicians and people were at odds with each other on how to replace the monarchy. Australia on this matter was now in limbo.

NOTES

QUESTION 1: WHY DID ABORIGINES NOT BECOME FARMERS?

p. 9, 'The archaeologist Rhys Jones ...': Rhys Jones, 'Fire-Stick Farming', *Australian Natural History*, vol. 16, 1969, pp. 224–231.

p. 10, 'People farmed in 1788 ...': Bill Gammage, *The Biggest Estate on Earth*, Allen & Unwin, Sydney, 2011, p. 281.

p. 11, 'The legal team running...': B. A. Keon-Cohen, 'The *Mabo* Litigation: A personal and procedural account', *Melbourne University Law Review*, vol. 24, no. 3, 2000, pp. 918–919.

p. 16, 'The Advance of the Austronesians' (map): Andrew Pawley, 'The Austronesian Dispersal', page 252 of *Examining the Farming/Language Dispersal Hypothesis*, edited by Peter Bellwood & Colin Renfrew, McDonald Institute for Archaeological Research, University of Cambridge, 2002.

p. 16, 'How much the spread of farming...': Contrast Peter Bellwood, *First Farmers: The origins of agricultural societies*, Blackwell, Malden MA, 2005, with Graeme Barker, *The Agricultural Revolution in Pre-History*, Oxford University Press, Oxford, 2006.

p. 16–17, 'Blainey calls the Aborigines …': see chapter 13 of Geoffrey Blainey, *The Triumph of the Nomads*, Macmillan, Melbourne, 1975.

p. 18, 'Their leader, Vincent Lingiari, said …': Frank Hardy, *Unlucky Australians*, Rigby, Adelaide, 1976, p. 90.

p. 19, Professor Barker's List: Barker, *The Agricultural Revolution*, p. 383.

p. 20, 'One proposed explanation …': Charles B. Heiser, *Seed to Civilization* (second edition), Freeman, San Francisco, 1981, pp. 27–28.

p. 22–23, 'Captain Cook had been …': Manning Clark, *Sources of Australian History*, Oxford University Press, London, 1957, p. 54.

p. 23, 'An anthropologist studying …': A. K. Chase, 'Northern Australia', in *Foraging and Farming*, edited by David R. Harris & Gordon C. Hillman, Unwin Hyman, London, 1989, p. 52.

p. 24, 'A Wiradjuri man …': Richard Broome, *Aboriginal Australians: A history since 1788*, Allen & Unwin, Sydney, 2010, p. 32.

p. 25, 'The Aborigines were proud …': Ann McGrath, *'Born in the Cattle'*, Allen & Unwin, Sydney, 1987, pp. 174–175.

QUESTION 2: HOW DID A PENAL COLONY CHANGE PEACEFULLY TO A DEMOCRACY?

This chapter draws on my *Convict Society and its Enemies* and *The Strange Birth of Colonial Democracy*. These have been reprinted together in *Freedom on the Fatal Shore* (Black Inc., Melbourne, 2008), which includes references and replies to those who take a contrary view of New South Wales. See also my 'The Convict Colony', in Norval Morris & David J. Rothman (eds), *The Oxford History of the Prison*, Oxford University Press, New York, 1995.

QUESTION 3: WHY WAS AUSTRALIA
SO PROSPEROUS SO EARLY?

p. 59, 'Australia had the highest …': Ian W. McLean, *Why Australia Prospered*, Princeton University Press, Princeton, 2013, pp. 11–12.

p. 63, 'As Grace Karskens reminds us …': Grace Karskens, *The Colony: A history of early Sydney*, Allen & Unwin, Sydney, 2009, pp. 175–177.

p. 65, 'For the years 1788–1822 …': N. G. Butlin, *Forming a Colonial Economy: Australia 1810–1850*, Cambridge University Press, Melbourne, 1994, p. 69.

p. 65, 'There was outright fraud …': Butlin, *Forming a Colonial Economy*, p. 66.

p. 67, 'Here distance was not a handicap …': Geoffrey Blainey, *The Tyranny of Distance*, Sun Books, Melbourne, 1966; see Chapter 5.

p. 68, 'Labour costs were kept down …': Graham J. Abbott, *The Pastoral Age: A re-examination*, Macmillan, Melbourne, 1971, p. 106.

p. 69, 'Australia, as its greatest …': W. K. Hancock, *Australia*, Jacaranda, Brisbane, 1961 [1930], p. 20.

p. 70, 'explosive colonisation': James Belich, *Replenishing the Earth: The settler revolution and the rise of the Anglo-world, 1783–1939*, Oxford University Press, Oxford, 2009, p. 179.

p. 70, 'The open grasslands …': For the contrast with Argentina, see my 'La sociedad rural y la politica en Australia, 1850–1930', in J. Fogarty, E. Gallo & H. Diegue (eds), *Argentina y Australia*, Instituto Torcuato Di Tella, Buenos Aires, 1979, reproduced in part as 'Transformation on the Land' in my *Sense and Nonsense in Australian History* (Black Inc., Melbourne, 2006). See also McLean, *Why Australia Prospered*, passim.

p. 73, 'When news of the gold finds …': John Woodland, 'Company Mining in the Australian Gold Rush', PhD thesis, La Trobe University, 2009.

p. 78, 'Latter-day economists …': H. M. Boot, 'Government and the Colonial Economies', *Australian Economic History Review*, vol. 38, no. 1, 1998, pp. 74–101; Lionel Frost, 'Government and the Colonial Economies: An alternative view', *Australian Economic History Review*, vol. 40, no. 1, 2000, pp. 71–85; and H. M. Boot, 'Government and the Colonial Economies: A reply to Frost', *Australian Economic History Review*, vol. 40, no. 1, 2000, pp. 86–91.

p. 82, 'It was in this period …': Ian W. McLean, 'Australian Economic Growth in Historical Perspective', *Economic Record*, vol. 80, no. 250, 2004, pp. 334–335.

p. 84, 'In Australia by 1890 …': Raymond Markey, *The Making of the Labor Party in New South Wales 1880–1900*, New South Wales University Press, Sydney, 1988, p. 140; Stuart Macintyre, *A Concise History of Australia* (second edition), Cambridge University Press, Melbourne, 2004, p. 124.

QUESTION 4: WHY DID THE AUSTRALIAN COLONIES FEDERATE?

This chapter draws on my *The Sentimental Nation: The making of the Australian Commonwealth* (Oxford University Press, Melbourne, 2001); my chapter 'Women and History' in *Sense and Nonsense in Australian History* (Black Inc., Melbourne, 2006); and my paper 'The Chinese and Federation', in *After the Rush: Regulation, participation, and Chinese communities in Australia, 1860–1940*, edited by Sophie Couchman, John Fitzgerald & Paul Macgregor (*Otherland*, vol. 9, 2004).

p. 113, 'No motive power …': Clark, *Sources of Australian History*.

p. 120, 'In an influential textbook …': L. F. Crisp, *The Parliamentary Government of the Commonwealth of Australia*, Longmans Green, London, 1949 (later reissued as *Australian National Government*).

QUESTION 5: WHAT EFFECT DID CONVICT ORIGINS
HAVE ON NATIONAL CHARACTER?

p. 122–23, 'The best antidote to this view …': Henry Reynolds, '"That Hated Stain": The aftermath of transportation in Tasmania', *Historical Studies*, vol. 14, no. 53, 1969, pp. 19–31.

p. 124–25, 'William Howitt, a traveller …': William Howitt, *Land, Labour and Gold*, Lowden, Kilmore, 1972 [1855], pp. 188–189, 310.

p. 125, 'It is possible in Britain itself …': See Terry Coleman, *The Railway Navvies*, Penguin, Harmondsworth, 1965.

p. 126–27, 'When George Orwell described …': George Orwell, 'The Lion and the Unicorn', in *The Penguin Essays of George Orwell*, p. 147.

p. 128–29, '"One marked difference …"': Frank Crowley, *Colonial Australia 1875–1900*, Nelson, Melbourne, 1980, p. 33.

p. 129–30, 'As an 1850 British verse …': F. G. Clarke, *The Land of Contrarieties*, Melbourne University Press, Melbourne, 1977, p. 170.

p. 130, 'When the crowd …': *Sydney Morning Herald*, 10 February 1879.

p. 130, 'In 1942 Winston Churchill …': Graham Freudenberg, *Churchill and Australia*, Macmillan, Sydney, 2008, p. 1.

p. 130, 'In 1899 a well-intentioned …': *Sydney Morning Herald*, 11 May 1899.

p. 133–35, 'A Nation Is Born': *Sydney Morning Herald*, 8 May 1915. Ashmead-Bartlett's wording, punctuation and arrangement are different in the *Argus* of the same date, which is reproduced in Frank Crowley, *Modern Australia in Documents, vol. 1, 1901–1939*, Wren, Melbourne, 1973, pp. 234–235.

p. 135, 'New Zealand was not so desperate …': See my *The Sentimental Nation*, pp. 221–222.

p. 137–38, 'Dennis defended them in verse …': C. J. Dennis, *The Moods of Ginger Mick*, Angus & Robertson, Sydney (editions post-1918).

p. 139, 'If you are tired of this old theme …': Les Murray, *The Quality of Sprawl*, Duffy & Snellgrove, Sydney, 1999, pp. 26–28.

QUESTION 6: WHY WAS THE POSTWAR MIGRATION PROGRAMME A SUCCESS?

This chapter draws on my essays 'Australia's Absurd History' (in *Sense and Nonsense in Australian History*) and 'Managing Difference' and 'More or Less Diverse' (in *Looking for Australia*); James Jupp (ed.), *The Australian People: An encyclopedia of the nation, its people and their origins*, Angus & Robertson, Sydney, 1988; and John Lack & Jacqueline Templeton, *Bold Experiment: A documentary history of Australian immigration since 1945*, Oxford University Press, Melbourne, 1995.

p. 140–41, 'It was easy to describe …': John S. Western, *Social Inequality in Australian Society*, Macmillan, Melbourne, 1983, p. 257.

p. 142, 'Recently, three migration experts …': Andrew Markus, Peter McDonald & James Jupp, *Australia's Immigration Revolution*, Allen & Unwin, Sydney, 2009.

p. 142–43, 'In his textbook he calls it …': Jock Collins, *Migrant Hands in a Distant Land*, Pluto Press, Sydney, 1988, pp. 195–196.

p. 144–45, 'To one Irish Catholic rebel …': Margaret Kiddle, *Caroline Chisholm*, Melbourne University Press, Melbourne, 1990, pp. 195–196.

p. 146, 'as the third verse …': Frank Crowley, *Colonial Australia 1875–1900*, Nelson, Melbourne, 1980, p. 48.

p. 148–49, 'But the Irish Catholics came to adore …': Patrick O'Farrell, *The Irish in Australia*, New South Wales University Press, Kensington, 1986, p. 263.

p. 149, 'Forty thousand people packed …': *Argus*, 10 April 1918, p. 9.

p. 151, 'As the English novelist …': D. H. Lawrence, *Kangaroo*, Penguin, London, 1950, p. 27.

p. 152, 'I have written on this topic …': John Hirst, 'The Distinctiveness of Australian Democracy', *Papers on Parliament*, no. 42, December 2004, p. 124.

p. 153–54, 'As one Jewish refugee reported …': Eugene Kamenka, 'Australia Made Me', *Quadrant*, October 1993, p. 26.

p. 154, 'To give Professor Collins …': Collins, *Migrant Hands in a Distant Land*, p. 210.

p. 162, 'The demographer Charles Price …': James Jupp (ed.), *The Australian People*, pp. 127–128 (emphasis added).

QUESTION 7: WHY IS AUSTRALIA NOT A REPUBLIC?

This chapter draws on Mark McKenna, *The Captive Republic: A history of republicanism in Australia, 1788–1996*, Cambridge University Press, Melbourne, 1996; and on my own *The Sentimental Nation*, 'Labor and Conscription' and 'Towards the Republic' (in *Sense and Nonsense in Australian History*), and 'Was Curtin the Best Prime Minister?' (in *Looking for Australia*).

p. 178, 'In 1900 Alfred Deakin …': Alfred Deakin (edited by J. A. LaNauze), *Federated Australia*, Melbourne University Press, Melbourne, 1968, p. 8.

p. 180, 'As Neville Meaney says …': Neville Meaney, *Australia and World Crisis 1914–1923*, Sydney University Press, Sydney, 2009; see chapters 5 and 6.

p. 181, 'The Motherland's Misalliance': *Bulletin*, 1 March 1902.

p. 185–86, 'Arthur Balfour, a British elder statesman …': W. J. Hudson & M. P. Sharp, *Australian Independence: Colony to reluctant kingdom*, Melbourne University Press, Melbourne, 1988, p. 93.

p. 187, 'On his return to Australia ...': *Sydney Morning Herald*, 27 May 1941.

p. 188, 'Curtin withdrew it and ...': James Curran, *Curtin's Empire*, Cambridge University Press, Melbourne, 2011, p. 14.

p. 190, 'A "new nationalism" emerged ...': This is discussed in James Curran & Stuart Ward, *The Unknown Nation: Australia after empire*, Melbourne University Press, Melbourne, 2010.

p. 192, 'Immediately it had an effect ...': Opinion polls on the republic are recorded and analysed in Malcolm Turnbull, *Fighting for the Republic*, Hardie Grant Books, Melbourne, 1999.

p. 193, 'The expert authors ...': W. J. Hudson & M. P. Sharp, *Australian Independence: Colony to reluctant kingdom*, Melbourne University Press, Melbourne, 1988, p. 138.

p. 194, 'He boasted that the republic ...': Paul Kelly, *The March of Patriots*, Melbourne University Press, Melbourne, 2009, p. 177.

p. 197, 'Half those who voted "no" ...': Turnbull, *Fighting for the Republic*, p. 241.

INDEX

Lightning Source UK Ltd.
Milton Keynes UK
UKOW02f1306181114

241789UK00016B/563/P